Speaking of Empire and Resistance

Speaking of Empire and Resistance

CONVERSATIONS WITH TARIQ ALI

TARIQ ALI AND
DAVID BARSAMIAN

THE NEW PRESS

NEW YORK
LONDON

Requests for permission to reproduce selections from this book should be mailed to:
Permissions Department, The New Press, 38 Greene Street, New York, NY 10013

Published in the United States by The New Press, New York, 2005
Distributed by W. W. Norton & Company, Inc., New York

Library of Congress Cataloging-in-Publication Data
Ali, Tariq.
Speaking of empire and resistance : conversations with Tariq Ali /
Tariq Ali and David Barsamian.
p. cm.
ISBN 1-56584-954-X (pbk.)
1. Ali, Tariq—Interviews.   2. United States—Foreign relations—21st century.
3. World politics—21st century.   4. Imperialism.
I. Barsamian, David.   II. Title.
E895.A42   2005
2004051369

The New Press was established in 1990 as a not-for-profit alternative to the large,
commercial publishing houses currently dominating the book publishing industry.
The New Press operates in the public interest rather than for private gain, and is
committed to publishing, in innovative ways, works of educational, cultural, and
community value that are often deemed insufficiently profitable.
www.thenewpress.com

Composition by dix!

Printed in Canada

2   4   6   8   10   9   7   5   3   1

Contents

1

The Empire Strikes Back

A Pakistani general once told you, "Pakistan was the condom that the Americans needed to enter Afghanistan. We've served our purpose and they think we can be just flushed down the toilet." That was in the 1980s, when the United States and Pakistan funded and armed the mujahedeen to defeat the godless Soviet Union. Is the United States again using Pakistan as a condom?

I think the Americans fished out the same condom but found it had too many holes in it. So they supplied a new one, and they've gone in again. This time they couldn't use the Pakistani army, since the Pakistani army created the Taliban and propelled it to victory. It could hardly be expected to kill its own offspring. The U.S. forced the Pakistani army to withdraw its support, which it did reluctantly. But it had to. Once Pakistani support

This interview, conducted in November 2001, first appeared in *The Progressive* (January 2002).

was withdrawn from the Taliban, they collapsed like a house of cards, though one hard-line faction will probably carry on in the mountains for a bit. The Islamabad faction will do what it's told and might be used by Washington if necessary.

Most Americans may not know the history of Pakistani–U.S. support for the Taliban. In a talk you gave in late September, you said, "People are taught to forget history." What did you mean?

In the West, since the collapse of Communism and the fall of the Soviet Union, the one discipline both the official and unofficial cultures have united in casting aside is history. It's as if history has become subversive. The past has too much knowledge embedded in it, and therefore it's best to forget it and start anew. But as everyone is discovering, you can't do this to history; it refuses to go away. If you try to suppress it, it reemerges in a horrific fashion. That's essentially what's been going on.

It's a total failure of the Western imagination that the only enemy they can see is Adolf Hitler. This is something that started during the Suez War of 1956, what I call the first oil war. Gamal Abdel Nasser, the nationalist leader of Egypt, was described by British prime minister Anthony Eden as an Egyptian Hitler. Then it carried on like that. Saddam Hussein became Hitler when he was no longer a friend of the West. Then Milosevic became Hitler. The Croatian fascists and the special SS-recruited brigades in Bosnia and Kosovo that had fought for Hitler are rarely mentioned. Now al Qaeda and the Taliban are portrayed as Islamo-fascists. The strong implication is that Osama bin Laden is a Hitler, even though he has no state power at all. It's a grotesque assertion if you think about it seriously. In reality, the only player still in this Afghan game who was soft on the Nazis is King Zahir Shah, who occupied the Afghan throne during the Second World War. He hoped the Germans would defeat the British in India, and that he, having collaborated, might share part of the spoils!

The reason they can get away with such crude caricatures is that history has been totally downplayed. We have populations now in the West with a very short memory span. One reason is that the last fifteen years has seen a big decline in television coverage of the rest of the world. At the same time there's been a series of idealized movies and endless documentaries on the Second World War. History, when they cover it at all, is ancient history, and they sensationalize even that. Recent history is virtually ignored on television. If you see what passes as the news on the networks in the United States, there's virtually no coverage of the rest of the world; not even of neighboring countries like Mexico or continents like Latin America. It's essentially a very provincial culture that breeds ignorance. Such ignorance is very useful in times of war because you can whip up a rapid rage in ill-informed populations and go to war against almost any country. That is a very frightening process.

Contrast the last wars of the twentieth century with the first war of the twenty-first century.

One difference is that the previous wars were fought by genuine coalitions. The United States was the dominant power in these coalitions, but it had to get other people on its side. In both the Gulf War and in Kosovo, the U.S. had to obtain the agreement of others before it moved forward. In the Afghanistan war, the first conflict of the twenty-first century, the United States just did as it pleased, not caring about who it antagonized, not caring about the effects on neighboring regions. I don't think it's too bothered with what happens afterwards, otherwise it would be more worried about the Northern Alliance. The U.S. is telling the Northern Alliance to kill Taliban prisoners. It's a total breach of all known conventions of war. Western television networks aren't covering this, but Arab networks have shown massacres of prisoners. All we see are scenes that are deliberately created for the Western media.

All these wars are similar in the way ideology is being used. It's the ideology of so-called humanitarian intervention. We don't want to do this, but we're doing it for the sake of the people who live there. This is, of course, a sleight of hand because all sorts of people live there, and, by and large, the intervention is to help one faction and not the other and above all to serve Western interests: strategic, political, and economic. In the case of Afghanistan, they didn't even pretend to be even-handed humanitarians. It was essentially a crude war of revenge designed largely to appease the U.S. public. In Canada in mid-November, I was debating Charles Krauthammer on *CounterSpin* on CBC: I said it was a war of revenge, and he said, Yeah, it is. So what? The more hard-line people, who are also more realistic, are quite open about this.

And the United States has perfected the manipulation involved. The media plays a big role.

In what way?

During the first Gulf War, journalists challenged government news managers and insisted they wouldn't just accept the official version of events. It seems that with the war in the Balkans and now the war against terror, journalists have accepted the official version. Journalists go to press briefings at the Ministry of Defense in London or the Pentagon in Washington, and no critical questions are posed at all. It's just a news-gathering operation, and the fact that the news is being controlled by governments who are waging war doesn't seem to worry many journalists too much. Embedded journalism is simply accepted. All the ideological broadsides against the Soviet media have long been forgotten. Judith Miller of the *New York Times* could have been a senior *Pravda* correspondent in the Brezhnev era.

The task of objective coverage really does devolve to alternative networks of information and education. The Internet has been an invaluable development. I wonder how we would do without it. But still, the independent news sources can't compete with the power and wealth of those five or six large companies who own the mainstream media today.

Tony Blair has occupied center stage in the war on terrorism. What accounts for his enthusiasm for the war?

Blair does it to get attention. He does it to strike a posture and prance around on the world stage, pretending that he is the leader of a big imperial power when, in fact, he's the leader of a medium-sized country in Northern Europe. I think Clinton certainly liked using him. But the Bush administration didn't take him that seriously at first. Later he became a vital prop in the new imperial offensive. He's nothing more than a second-rate actor with a third-rate mind.

Noam Chomsky points out that Britain did not bomb Boston and New York, where major IRA supporters and financial networks are located.

I think Noam's right. But to even raise the point goes to show that Britain isn't an imperial power and the United States is. The United States is now The Empire. There isn't an empire; there's The Empire, and that empire is the United States. It's very interesting that this war is not being fought by the NATO high command. NATO has been totally marginalized. The "coalition against terrorism" means the United States; it does not want anyone else to interfere with its strategy. When the Germans offered 2,000 soldiers, Rumsfeld said he had never asked for them. It was quite amazing for him to say this in public.

In a recent article, you cited a poem by the tenth-century secular Arab poet Abu al-Ala al-Maarri:

And where the Prince commanded, now the shriek,
Of wind is flying through the court of state;
"Here," it proclaims, "there dwelt a potentate,
Who would not hear the sobbing of the weak."

Talk about "the sobbing of the weak."

The sobbing of the weak today is the sobbing of the victims of neoliberal policies. They number billions of people across the world. These are the people who leave their countries. These are the people who cling onto the belly of a plane leaving Africa for Europe, not caring if they are killed in the process, and many of them are. Their desperation is the result of globalization. The question is, will the weak be able to organize themselves to bring about changes or not? Will the weak develop a sufficient internal political strength to ever challenge the rulers? People are increasingly beginning to feel that democracy itself is being destroyed by this latest phase of globalization, and that politics doesn't matter because it changes nothing. This is a very dangerous situation on the global level because when this happens you begin to see acts of terrorism. Terrorism emanates from weakness, not strength. It is the sign of despair.

Al-Maarri was a great skeptic poet. He wrote a parody of the Koran, and his friends would tease him and say, "Al-Maarri, but no one recites your Koran." And he said, "Yes, but give me time. Give me time. If people recite it for twenty years it will become as popular as the other one." It was a good moment in Islam when people were challenging authority at every level. Very different from the world we live in now, incidentally. Islamists, like many Protestant Puritans, have become scriptural literalists. They want to avoid any real discussion of Islamic history and retreat to the text.

And in this world, the United States is projecting a long war on terrorism. They're talking about it lasting for ten or fifteen years, and involving up to sixty countries. The Bush administration reminds us almost on a daily basis that the war on terrorism is still in its earliest stages. What are the implications of that?

The main implication is a remapping of the world in line with American policy and interests. Natural resources are limited, and the United States wants to make sure that its own population is kept supplied. The principle effect of this will be for the United States to control large parts of the oil which the world possesses. There are some people who say this war was fought because of oil. I don't believe that. But that doesn't mean the war won't be used to reassert American economic hegemony in the region, and oil is a central aspect of this.

A big problem for the United States in the Middle East is that Iraq and Syria are potential threats to Israel just by the very fact of their existence. Iraq also sits on a great deal of oil, and as that cutthroat Henry Kissinger once said, "Why should we let the Arabs have the oil?" Since Israel is the central ally of the United States in the region, the U.S. would like to weaken its potential opponents. Attacking Iraq, and possibly even Syria, is one way to do that. This is a policy fraught with danger for those who carry it out because it totally excludes the reaction of ordinary people. Could there be mass explosions? And if there are, then you will see countries like Saudi Arabia going under. Few would weep if the Saudi royal family were overthrown, but would matters improve if it were replaced by a U.S. protectorate or the U.S. disguised as the UN? Other corrupt sheikdoms, like the United Arab Emirates, would crumble as well. Then what will the U.S. do? Have the Israelis acting as guardians of oil in the whole region? That will involve permanent guerrilla warfare. Or will they have American and European troops guarding these regions? That, too, would mean a prolonged guerrilla conflict. The only way they'll be able to rule is by killing large numbers of people who live there.

What about Iraq?

If they attack Iraq in the next phase, it could create big problems for them. I'm confident that in Europe the antiwar movement would mushroom. The Arab world could really explode. That is what their close allies in Saudi Arabia and Egypt are telling them: Do not attack Iraq. The coalition will break up; even Turkey is saying that it will not be party to an attack on Iraq. But if they do decide to go down that route, the world will become a very unpredictable and very dangerous place. The one thing that it will not do is curb terrorism. It will increase terrorism, because the more countries you destroy, the more the people will seek revenge.

After flirting with neoisolationism, the U.S. is now deciding it wants to run the world. The U.S. should come out openly and say to the world, "We are the only imperial power, and we're going to rule you, and if you don't like it you can lump it." American imperialism has always been the imperialism that has been frightened of speaking its name. Now it's beginning to do so. In a way, it's better. We know where to kneel.

2

Imperialism: Then and Now

*Imperialism is not a word often used in polite discourse in the
United States.*

In all my travels throughout the United States, I've
always found that very strange—it's a word Americans
don't like. Partially this is because of the Cold War and
partially because it challenges the self-image of the
United States. But it's a word that was used a lot when
the British Empire was dominant. Liberal magazines in
the U.S. were constantly attacking the British Empire;
on the eve of the Second World War, a series of articles in
the *New Republic* suggested there was little basis on which
to choose between the British Empire and Hitler. This
hostility to the British Empire had long existed because of
the origins of the American state, and therefore Ameri-

This interview, conducted in January 2003, first appeared in *Z Magazine* (April 2003) and
was broadcast on *Alternative Radio*.

cans were very reluctant to accept that their own country had all the makings of an empire from the start. They assumed that an empire consisted of colonies abroad that were ruled and staffed by people you sent from the imperial country, whether it was Britain in India, France in Algeria, Germany in Namibia, or Belgium in the Congo. And they said, "Well, we don't do it like that."

It's true that the United States didn't do it like that, but it did it nevertheless. Look at its internal expansion. First, it conquered and destroyed the indigenous population. Then it eyed its neighbors, gobbled up bits of Mexico, and incorporated them into the United States. The United States did something very similar to czarist Russia: ingesting nearby countries and making them part of the Russian empire. Here, the conquered territory became part of the United States of America.

Then the Americans found a different way of moving forward. The American empire worked very quickly to control Latin America in the nineteenth century and the early twentieth century, according to the Monroe Doctrine. The Monroe Doctrine proclaimed: "Latin America is our backyard. We're not going to tolerate any trouble there." Look at the number of military interventions carried out, first in the Central American republics, then throughout Latin America. These were carried out to defend American corporate interests. This is when the term "banana republics" came into being, because American companies were going into these countries backed by the

Marines—securing these territories for the corporations, so that American capitalism could grow and triumph.

But for a long period the U.S. kept to its own sphere.
What led them to reach out further was not so much the
need for colonies—they didn't need colonies, given the
size and scale of the United States itself and the natural
resources it possessed, and in any case, they already dominated South America. What forced them to move out
(the Philippines was exceptional) was not even the First
World War. What compelled them to act was the Russian
Revolution. There is a very interesting parallel: At the
same time as the Russian Revolution was taking place,
Woodrow Wilson decided it was time for a major U.S. intervention, because American planners began to fear that
the threat to capitalist interests in Europe might also
threaten them in the long term. That's when they decided
they had to go international. They had been quite happy
to be a regional imperial power until then. This decision
basically changed the course of politics—both in the
United States and around the world.

It can be argued, of course, that this is a direction
they had to go in. The old empires were breaking up and
falling apart, and sooner or later new power had to
emerge. That new power was the United States of America. And the victory of the Russian Revolution meant that
it had a global enemy. Here was a country which challenged capitalism quite openly and said, "We want to cre-

ate a system which is better than yours." So for seventy years they fought that system politically, economically, and militarily. The final victory was achieved by forcing the Soviet Union to go on a completely unnecessary military spending binge to keep pace with the U.S. *The Economist* celebrated with a cover headline: "The Joys of Rearmament." The USSR wasn't invaded or defeated militarily. It imploded. That was a massive victory for capitalism and the United States.

To what extent is imperialism connected to, or derived from, capitalism? You mentioned Russian expansion; one could add that the Soviet Union also had dependent states.

Soviet expansion after the Second World War was— far from being economically exploitative—something they needed, geographically and militarily, to create a network of states that were part of their sphere of influence and part of their social/economic system, in order to hold the United States at bay. This was the result of the famous deal made with the Americans and the British at Yalta in 1945. Roosevelt and Churchill told Stalin: "You can have Poland, Hungary, Czechoslovakia. Yugoslavia should be fifty-fifty. Greece is ours, so if there is a revolutionary movement there, we'll crush it, and you stay out of it." That's how the whole deal was done.

But let's leave that aside, because it is largely of historical interest now. All the early empires were founded because of the need for capital to expand, the need for capital to find new markets. It was this struggle for markets that created the British Empire, the Dutch empire, the Belgian empire, the French empire. The First World War was a war fought over colonial expansion. Who would control the trade routes? Who would control the markets? Germany, which unified late and came to capitalism later than the other powers, decided it wanted its own empire. It felt that the way to get it was to defeat Britain, and then it could actually move forward. So this was the case in the past.

For a while this was disguised: while the Soviet Union and the Eastern Bloc existed, there was talk of imperialism, but by and large people in the West regarded the situation as a war against an enemy, which one of Reagan's speechwriters dubbed an evil empire. Now the slate is clean once again. We have the world before us: naked. We can see exactly what is going on. The September 2002 *National Security Strategy of the United States* put out by the Bush administration makes the situation crystal clear. They say the defense of free trade—i.e., free trade as we see it and according to rules that we make—is a holy moral principle. And in order to defend this, we are prepared to go to war. That has been the principle of all empires.

The difference between the American and previous empires is that the United States usually prefers to work through local compradors, local rulers who are on their side. They don't like ruling directly, because they know it's an enormous expense. Why send your own people out to run a country when you can find locals to do it? And that is how they've always operated. For example, during the occupation of Japan after the Second World War, they created a constitution, and MacArthur was like a viceroy. But they pulled out after a few years and let their local relays in Japan carry on, as they still do. The Japanese Liberal Democratic Party was created by the United States to do the job for them and did so effectively. Of course, there were U.S. troops stationed in Okinawa, just in case something went badly wrong.

And this is the way they do it. It's very interesting that even in the case of Afghanistan, which is now a colonial state, the U.S. didn't want to have their own people there pending a general election. They put a puppet, a former friend of the CIA and the Unocal oil company, Hamid Karzai, in power in Kabul. And he does the work for them, even though they can't leave him undefended and he wouldn't last too long if Western troops were withdrawn.

The question now posed is this: Who are the rivals of the United States, and how will it defend its interests against them? Europe is a rival, not politically or militarily but economically—not the European Union, because it is a weak entity, but countries like Germany and France, which are plausible economic rivals because their firms compete in the same markets as American companies. There is this notion today that, because of multinational capital, the nation-state has become irrelevant. I don't buy that for a minute. The multinationals certainly exist, but we know very clearly where their ownership lies. Halliburton and Bechtel, for instance, are based in the United States; some of their rivals are in Germany and France. The nation-state is still very important to defend the interests of these so-called multinationals. They are multinational only in terms of exploitation; in terms of their roots, they are tied to particular nation-states. And so this rivalry between the imperial economic interests of the United States and some of the European countries are clear and underlie the differences on Iraq.

And looking to the future, the U.S. sees the Far Eastern region—the united Korean peninsula, Japan, and China—as a combination that could be deadly if it ever got together economically, politically, and militarily. They fear that if this happened, within ten years this area would establish economic hegemony. American strategic policy is designed to keep these countries separate from each other. That's why the Bush regime is even now trying to stop Korean reunification: because they are fearful that a unified Korean peninsula with nuclear weapons would make the Japanese develop nuclear weapons. Then you would have three nuclear powers in the region: Japan, Korea, and China. And if that ever happened, I think the Americans would try and make these countries fight each other, because they are really fearful of any kind of union in this region. That would severely threaten their interests.

To be frank, most of Bush's supporters writing in the American press hardly make much of an effort to conceal these motivations. If you read Thomas Friedman's articles on the war in Iraq, this guy spells it out quite openly. He says, It's laughable to pretend it's not about oil; it's just that it's not only about oil. So they are no longer even trying to veil their real aims. They are saying, "This is the situation. We're the world's mightiest power. These are our economic interests, these are our strategic interests, and these are our geopolitical interests. And you'd better watch out, guys, because we're going to defend them." This is imperialism, different from the past, in a new situation. And in the war in Iraq, they will assert new, raw imperial power in a way they have not done before.

Walter Rodney, the important political thinker and writer from Guyana, talked about what he called "the local lackeys" of imperialism, something you've just touched upon. Tell me more about this class of collaborators who serve the metropolitan center.

This has been such a clear pattern throughout the twentieth century that we can follow it very closely. There was a long period in the middle of the century that saw the rise of nationalism, the rise of anticolonial movements, and the rise of national liberation movements against the old empires. But already, standing in the shadows behind the old empires, was the United States of America. As the old empires were going down, they were being replaced by American power.

What happened in the middle of the last century? The Korean War. A three-year war fought by the United States under the banner of the United Nations, in the course of which the industrially strong part of Korea—the north—was completely devastated. Not a single building was left standing. Its entire infrastructure was destroyed. And then both sides agreed to a cease-fire.

Next came the Vietnam War. First, the French were defeated in Vietnam. The United States was not prepared to allow that defeat and stepped in. And for the first time, American leaders thought of using nuclear weapons: John Foster Dulles, the secretary of state, suggested to Western allies and the French that perhaps nuclear force would be necessary to stop "these ants" crawling up the hills around Dien Bien Phu—the big battle where the French were defeated. By "these ants," Dulles meant the Vietnamese people; they could be destroyed.

I begin with these examples because without understanding the national movements and the role they played, we can't properly understand the role of the collaborators. The aim of the American empire was, by hook or by crook, to get rid of these governments; to maintain a nationalist pretense but put in power people who could posture as anticolonial nationalists while actually serving the needs of the great metropolitan empire.

How did they do this? They failed in Vietnam. They succeeded in dividing Korea. But they couldn't rule South Korea democratically, because no lackeys could be found who could be elected. So when you can't find lackeys who can be elected democratically, you put the army in power. They did exactly the same thing in Pakistan: A general election was planned for April 1959, which would have produced a government that would have withdrawn from the security pacts into which the U.S. had tied Pakistan. The Americans organized a coup d'état and put the military in power in October 1958 to pre-empt a general election.

The country which worried them the most in the middle of the last century was Indonesia, because it had the world's largest Communist party outside China and Russia, a party with a million members and an additional two million people organized in front organizations. The Communist Party had a big influence on the government and within the armed forces. So what did the Americans do? They organized one of the most dastardly actions we have seen since the Second World War, a military coup that put Suharto in power. Suharto then proceeded to kill a million people and wipe out the most powerful social movement in the country. The killings in the rural areas, where the Communists had organized the peasants, were horrendous. A million people dead, and as *Time* magazine put it, quite bluntly, it was the best news the West had had from Asia in a long time. It was a big victory. A dictator much more vicious than anything we have seen in Iraq came to power on a mountain of corpses, and in Suharto the Americans found a local collaborator who stayed in power until the end of the twentieth century. In 1975 he invaded East Timor, killed several hundred thousand people there. In Indonesia earlier he had physically exterminated the secular and radical opposition. Now many are surprised that the Islamists in Indonesia are so powerful, but this is because the Islamists are the people who were used in 1965 to kill Reds: Go and wipe them out. They're atheists, they're communists. Kill, kill, kill, kill. This is how collaborators are created.

In the most recent phase, following the end of the Cold War, the triumph of the United States and world capitalism has totally disarmed even semi-nationalist politicians, who said, "Now there is nothing else to do. Just work with them, serve them." This has led to a phenomenal growth in corruption all over the Third World, and not just there—in the First and Second Worlds as well. There has been massive corruption in politics, which has become part of corporate life. This has been the case in the States for some time, but it has recently begun to seep through. It's been very difficult in the last twenty years to get elected leaders who are prepared to fight for their own people and the rights of their own state.

We're doing this interview in Latin America, and this is a continent that has been in revolt for some time. We have seen the election of Hugo Chavez in Venezuela, the failure to topple Fidel Castro after forty years of the blockade, and the victory of Lula in Brazil, where we are sitting and talking. We have seen the triumph of Lucio Gutierrez in Ecuador; and in Bolivia, Evo Morales came very close to defeating the corporations' candidate. So we are seeing the stirrings of a new wave of what we might call sub-nationalism or proto-nationalism, which wants to resist but doesn't know how to resist. If a viable model was developed, it could spread elsewhere. But by and large, in Asia and Africa the regimes remain pliable.

This can't last forever. I think, curiously enough, that the war in Iraq, the occupation of Iraq, and the establishment of an American puppet government to replace Saddam so the oil can be shared as a war trophy, is bound to create a resistance sooner or later. It may take four years; it may take ten years. We don't know. But it will happen. In that sense, the American empire is no different from other empires. It is slowly sowing the seeds of the forces that will one day confront it.

But the confrontation also has to come from within America itself. It's very interesting that Seattle was where the antiglobalization movement was born. We should re-member that the world's first Anti-Imperialist League was founded in Chicago in 1898, by a group of Ameri-cans, Mark Twain foremost among them. They were reacting to the American occupation of the Philippines, where the Americans cut a deal with the Spanish very similar to the one they would later strike with the French in Vietnam. You get out of the Philippines. There will be some mock battle—fake wrestling, as we used to call it in our part of the world—and then we will take over. The Americans took control and they oversaw the crushing of the nationalist movement. Within a year the Anti-Imperialist League established in Chicago had a quarter of a million members in thirty different cities, a time when there was no communism, no social enemies like that on a world scale, but imperialism still existed. And brave and intelligent American citizens could see that it existed.

I honestly think that the time has come for the heirs of Mark Twain and the other pioneers of that anti-imperialist league to get together and create such a body once again, because American imperialism is much more dangerous now; its military power is virtually unchallengeable because of the technological advancements that have taken place. It's really a vital step, to establish an organization that will fight the empire morally from within its own heart. I'm very keen that this happen.

Nineteenth-century European imperialism was predicated on racism: bringing civilization and Christianity to the benighted natives. That was then. What about now? What factor does racism play in imperialism?

Racism was the basis of the old empires, and yet there is a similarity between old and new. The propaganda and the rhetoric behind the new wars of "humanitarian intervention" is very interesting. When they went into the Balkans, they used this rhetoric. I was reminded then that the propaganda of the British as they took a large chunk of the African continent also invoked humanitarian intervention. We are going in there, the British said, basically to destroy slavery—this from a country which had profited enormously from slavery. Most of the big fortunes and the big country estates that people go and look at in Britain were built on slavery. The slave trade played a very big part in the formation—economically, socially, and culturally—of the British ruling class in the eighteenth century and the early years of the nineteenth. The present calls for humanitarian intervention remind me of that a bit. But the racist motive has declined. It's not used that much; in fact, they're trying to bend over backwards to avoid using it, because they know it's quite explosive.

However, you can't deny that an underlying feeling of white superiority exists. I'll give you a concrete example: Consider the tragedy of September 11, when lots of civilians were killed in New York and Washington. The whole world was encouraged to weep for them in public, or at least that was the general mode of the media. Why? Because they were citizens of the United States of America. When Afghan citizens are killed by indiscriminate bombings, by so-called accidental bombings—as in the bombing of a wedding that took place because revelers were firing a few shots there and some American soldier thought, "Oh, God, we're being attacked. Go ahead and bomb the shit out of them." Or the deaths which are now taking place from starvation. These deaths don't count for much. No one will ever build a monument for the Afghan civilians who died in the bombing raids. This was just a crude war of revenge, as I called it at the time.

Why are Afghan lives less important? Because underlying all this rhetoric remains the belief that we are a superior nation, a superior race, and a superior people.

Look at the cavalier way that casualties in Iraq are discussed. An Iraqi friend of mine attended a conference organized by the State Department and its favorite Iraqis, to which he hadn't been invited. "What shocked me," he told me later, "was the way they were discussing casualties—how many civilian deaths would be acceptable." He said the figure the Iraqis and the Americans were discussing amongst themselves was 250,000—it shouldn't go above that. A quarter of a million civilian deaths are acceptable? Three thousand deaths are not acceptable in the United States of America, but a quarter of a million Iraqi deaths are acceptable. Is that not the most grotesque demonstration that the lives of these poor Arabs don't matter a damn? Today racism takes a different form than it did in the old empires, but it's still there.

In 1996 Madeleine Albright, then the U.S. ambassador to the United Nations, was asked about the impact of sanctions on Iraq, specifically the deaths of 500,000 Iraqi children. "Is the price worth it?" she was asked. And she answered, "We think the price is worth it."

That is one of the most shocking statements made by a senior American politician or leader since the Second World War. It's amazing that this didn't create mayhem in the United States. If Lyndon Johnson in 1968 or Richard Nixon in 1970 had made such a statement—that killing two million Vietnamese was worth it—there would have been absolute pandemonium. People would have been rushing to lay siege to the White House, demonstrating and saying, "Withdraw your words." The fact that Madeleine Albright said this on CBS to Lesley Stahl and was not reprimanded for it by Clinton is shocking. The official line was, "Saddam is responsible for those deaths." But let's leave that aside for a moment. That's not what Albright was asked. Stahl suggested to Albright that the sanctions had cost 500,000 children's lives in Iraq, and Albright said, that's a price worth paying. What can one say to a politician with such a brazen disregard for human life? I know people hate to hear it, but this is the sort of rhetoric used by the Third Reich in the 1930s— the death of many people is no big deal. They're *Untermenschen*. They're not like us. These are different people, and their lives don't concern us. We hear the same sort of rhetoric attempting to blame the victims for what's done to them. It's quite staggering. It's not the case that the figure of half a million was pulled out of the air by CBS. It's the official United Nations figure, supplied by UN organizations that have been in Iraq.

The genocidal impact of sanctions on Iraq forced two senior United Nations officials, Denis Halliday and Hans von Sponeck, to resign in disgust. Why did they resign? Because they were crazed radicals, or Islamists? They were decent, liberal human beings who could not tolerate what was being done in the name of the United Nations to the people of Iraq. If there were any justice in this world, Albright, Clinton, Blair, and the other politicians who pushed these sanctions through would be tried before a criminal court. The sanctions clearly failed to weaken the regime; all they did was make the people more dependent on it. Iraq was denied the right to import basic equipment to clean water and to repair the sewage systems.

This is where we see empires at their worst, and this one in particular at its worst. Look at the worst atrocities of the British Empire in India, like the Jallianwala Bagh episode in 1919, where they killed several hundred people in an afternoon, or the deliberately organized famines that killed hundreds of thousands of poor peasants, as depicted in the cinema of the late Satyajit Ray. Several hundred people, and there was an outcry all over the world. When King Leopold of Belgium started killing lots of

Congolese people, there was another massive outcry. Arthur Conan Doyle wrote a book called *The Crime of the Congo,* which sold 200,000 copies in two months. There was a massive worldwide campaign against those massacres. Today it's almost as if the world has gone to sleep; they're so comfortable and secure in Europe and North America that the deaths of ordinary civilians don't matter a damn—they all serve some cause. And I put it to you that the cause they serve is the cause of the American empire.

Talk about the role of the media in shaping and forming public opinion. For example, the American media constantly suggest that Saddam Hussein represents a grave threat to the United States. Can you discuss the contrast between the media in the United States and in Europe?

There is indeed a difference. What really astounds me in the United States is the lack of television coverage of the rest of the world. It is almost as if the only way they can teach people geography is by going and bombing countries. You don't know where Afghanistan is? It's here, look, we're bombing it. You don't know where Iraq is? It's here. We're going to bomb it, and then you will know where it is. You have a population which is not informed or educated by the media except when it is time for war. It's a process which can only be described as propaganda of the most disgusting sort. You don't allow people to think for themselves—you frighten them.

The notion that Saddam Hussein is a threat to the United States makes everyone in Europe laugh, including European politicians, who talk to the American leaders every day. They just laugh. Recently, I took part in a public debate in Berlin at a big theater, with one or two thousand people in the audience. I was debating Professor Ruth Wedgewood, an occasional adviser to Donald Rumsfeld. To my amazement she suddenly turned to the Germans, and she said, "I know why you are opposed to this war. It's because you're scared of Saddam." Afterwards, people said to me, "We were really taken aback by that. What does she mean?" I said, "This is what they say in the United States all the time. They frighten the people by convincing them that Saddam represents a real threat. And I'm staggered that they've begun to believe their own rhetoric." One of the audience members said to me, "For us this was not so much a political experience as an anthropological experience. This is a senior figure from the United States?" And there you see the big difference.

The media in the United States have degenerated. I can remember journalists covering the Vietnam War posing tough questions, asking, "What the hell is going on? Why are our boys suffering? Why is this happening?" That's all gone now. Wars are rarely, if ever, questioned by the big television panjandrums in the States, but the same is true with large numbers of television networks in Europe. The sharp difference is between the American and Western European print media. Consider the *New York Times*. It's not that it doesn't occasionally permit an op-ed column which is critical of established authority; but the overwhelming tenor of its reporting—its opinions, and who it allows and doesn't allow in its pages, is very much in step with the establishment. I like to joke sometimes—and it's only kind of a joke—that the *Times* is today the *Pravda* of the United States administration. Thomas Friedman, when he stands up at his pulpit, speaks in the voice of the empire. This is who we are, and watch out if you don't agree with us.

The funny thing is that these great so-called journalists travel all over the world, and sometimes they miss out on the most important struggles taking place because their eyes are just concentrated on what they need to report in their papers. The American media's coverage of the Israeli occupation of Palestine, to take one example, is so one-sided that it's almost as if the Palestinians were occupying Jewish lands and the Israelis were resisting a big force of Palestinians. This really depresses me to no end, because it's the exact opposite of reality.

In Europe the situation is slightly different. There are still newspapers that will publish critical articles. On Iraq, or on Palestine, there is critical coverage in the British, French, and Italian newspapers, of which you will find no equivalent in the United States, with the occasional exception of the *Los Angeles Times,* which sometimes publishes very critical stuff.

Such U.S. magazines as The Nation, In These Times, The Progressive, Z, *and all these new Web sites that have developed, such as indymedia.org, commondreams.org, or zmag .org, are providing alternative information.*

These alternative information networks have sprung up everywhere in the wake of Seattle, and this has been one of the most important developments in challenging the weight of the media. This is tremendous. It means that a small group of politically aware citizens anywhere in the world can access this material. This has been phenomenal, and I don't want to underestimate it. It has occasionally provided headaches for people like me, who get e-mails from all over the world. Your interview with me last year in *The Progressive* seemed to be reprinted on just about every Web site, and I got questions about it from sixty different countries. But that's a nice thing.

But we should not imagine this can somehow compete with the powers that be—that's a serious mistake. It's easy for us to get carried away and excited to think, "God, we broke the story first." That may be true, but we have to remember that the reach of the Internet can be very deceptive: just because it's on the Web doesn't mean that everyone gets it. And we have not been able to compete with mainstream media at all in television coverage.

In Genoa, the Italian police went into the Alternative Information Center and smashed it to bits. They were
scared because activists had television cameras and were
filming what was going on when Carlo Giuliani, one of
the protestors, was killed. But these alternative news
sources are still very important, because they break the
complete monopoly the authorities have.

One wonders how long they will even let us go on
with that, whether new restrictions will be imposed on
the Internet if they want to stop opposition and dissent.
Already we know that they can break into anyone's Web
site or e-mail—they're doing this. And sooner or later
they will possibly start blacking it out. So we should be on
the alert for that.

In some countries there are progressive daily newspapers that have managed to keep going. It's quite remarkable. In Norway, for example, there is *Klassekampen,*
class struggle. In Italy, there is *Il Manifesto.* When you talk
to the *Manifesto* editors, they say, "During times of crisis,
our circulation just shoots up. It's when people need alternatives." So I think the combination of these papers
and Web sites can be effective, but still, it's a drop in the
ocean. Then there is al-Jazeera, which has been effective
in showing alternative images from war zones, and its of-
fices in Kabul were bombed by the U.S.

In our Progressive *interview you briefly mentioned Tony
Blair. Talk more about him.*

The problem with Tony Blair is that he actually believes in the war on terrorism. He is a deeply conservative man; I have absolutely no doubt about that. He would have been a good leader of the Conservative Party. He's probably too right-wing for some conservatives, but he would have been perfectly at home there. Underlying Blair's politics, which very few people talk about, is a streak of Christian fundamentalism that goes very deep. He is the most religious leader Britian has had since [William] Gladstone. He has surrounded himself with a pseudo-Christian mafia, which is quite authoritarian in its social attitudes and beliefs. The new director-general of the BBC, Mark Thompson, is part of this pattern.

In terms of foreign policy, I think Blair decided as soon as he came into office that he was going to continue the deals Thatcher had made with Reagan. These deals—especially after the Malvinas [Falklands] conflict—have docked the British Ministry of Defense totally into the Pentagon. It's to the point now that when the Pentagon upgrades equipment or technology, the British Ministry of Defense, which doesn't need these upgrades, has to do so as well, because they're part of the same system.

Now the British political elites, both labor and conservative, are totally committed to this alliance. When Charles de Gaulle vetoed Britain's entry into the European Common Market, he used to say that Britain would always be an American Trojan horse in the European Union; how right he was. Blair likes to tell the Europeans, "I'm close to Bush; I can influence him." And he tells Bush, "It's important I'm in the European Union, because I can make sure that your views are properly defended there." That's the role Blair plays, but he is now seen as little more than the Trojan mule of the Pentagon.

Underlying Blair's servility to the United States is his own view of Britain. It is a medium-sized country. It no longer has an empire. The country has quite an exploitative deregulated system that attracts foreign capital because wages and taxes are low; this was Thatcher's achievement. Blair believes this has to be maintained, because he doesn't have any other vision. And one of the ways it can be maintained is by hanging alongside the United States in whatever they do, sharing part of the proceeds and remaining a loyal ally in Washington's eyes. It's classic—satraps used to do it in the days of the Roman Empire, making themselves more loyal to the empire than many people inside the empire itself, who could see the reality of what they were doing. That's what Blair has consciously decided he wants to be, a loyal satrap of the American empire.

I have to also tell you, because it would be one-sided not to do so, that he is hated by large numbers of people in Britain for doing this. Sections of the British establishment regard this sort of servility to the United States as debased, vulgar, and low. Within both the civil service and the military establishment there is a lot of nervousness and hostility to the war on Iraq. For the first time also in Britain you have a majority of public opinion against a war. So Blair is in some ways really putting his future on the line.

I mentioned Blair's Christianity and his belief that his future is tied with the United States, but there is one more salient feature: he's also a very greedy man. He's obsessed with money. He's always telling people at private dinner parties how being prime minister has meant that he's not earning as much money as he should be. When politicians combine piety on the one hand and greed on the other, and then are prepared to justify wars, they are internally very mixed-up. He has recently shown signs of cracking: when you look at him, he's looking very strained and tense. So the one good thing that might come from the war in Iraq is the end of Blair's political career. This is probably wishful thinking, but many people think that he won't stay long now. It's a strange phenomenon. He is unpopular and unspeakable, but appears untouchable.

The United States has been fervently looking for an opposi-tional force to replace the Soviet Union since its collapse. They tried Noriega in Panama, Qaddafi in Libya, and the Cali and Medellin drug cartels. Now they've zoomed in on Islam, a certain fundamentalist and militant variant of Islam, as the new arch-enemy.

They have indeed. The one thing on which the United States and many other countries can agree is that

Islamic fundamentalist terrorism is a bad thing, an enemy that has to be wiped out and destroyed. But where do you go from there? Because unless you understand what causes young people to sacrifice their own lives—what the process is and how to stop it—it will continue to happen. In order to justify infinite war, they have invented this enemy, which—I'm almost tired of pointing this out—they created themselves at the height of the Cold War to service their needs in Indonesia, Afghanistan, and the Arab world. The United States supported the people they now call their main enemies in order to destroy radical nationalist regimes that allied themselves to the Soviet Union and threatened American interests. Now these people have broken loose because the Americans dumped them. The Americans said, "We don't need you anymore," and the Islamists said, "You may not need us anymore, but we believe we have a role to play."

It's crazy to think of Islam as a monolith. It's just as divided as any other part of the world. As I pointed out to you before, the world's largest Muslim country, Indonesia, was also home to the largest Communist Party outside the communist states themselves. This used to shock people—"How did that happen?" they would ask. But developments like this took place all over the world during the twentieth century, even in the Islamic world. It has been the destruction of these oppositional currents that created the monster the United States now pretends is a massive enemy. How is al Qaeda a big enemy? At most they have two thousand to maybe four thousand members. No one has agreed on a precise number ensconced in different parts of the world, including parts of Europe and the United States of America. How come this can't be destroyed? It can be, but the problem is not al Qaeda. The problem is the conditions that drive young people to despair. That cannot be reversed so easily, and it will not stop unless the central problems in the Middle East—Palestine, Israel, what's being done to Iraq—are solved.

That's one reason why the war in Iraq, far from being a war against terrorism, should be called a war to promote terrorism, because the Arab world will feel our governments have let this happen. How are we going to respond when Baghdad, the historic city of Islamic civilization, the city of the caliphs and *The Thousand and One Nights,* is once again occupied by crusaders? That's what they will see. It is seen in the Arab world as a crusade for oil. And the reason they've made Islam the big enemy now is because oil lies beneath Islamic lands, which is an accident of geography and history. But the richest deposits of oil lie underneath Muslim lands. There is oil in Brunei, a Muslim country in Southeast Asia; Iraq has the second largest deposits of oil; Iran has oil; the Arabian peninsula has oil. If there was no oil underneath the Islamic world; if it was somewhere else—let's suppose all the oil or the bulk of the oil was in Africa—those countries would be the enemy. The West would be saying, "They are not proper Christians. They have never learned proper Christianity," or whatever. I think the reason that Islam is the enemy today is tied very closely to oil, to the need for the West to control this region forever. That's the plan.

Bernard Lewis has achieved almost iconic status in the West as an expert on Islam and Muslim thought. He wrote a famous essay for the Atlantic Monthly *in 1990 called "The Roots of Muslim Rage," in which he used the term "clash of civilizations." That term was picked up later by Harvard University professor Samuel Huntington, who wrote a book called* The Clash of Civilizations. *Now you have written a book called* The Clash of Fundamentalisms. *What do you think about this theory?*

Lewis's theory is largely based on a view of a world which I don't recognize. I grew up in the Muslim world and have traveled extensively throughout it. There is rage in the Muslim world, obviously, but the reasons for that rage are very clear. The reasons for the rage are the imposition of a settler state in the heart of the Arab world and the attempt to destroy the Palestinians and their identity. That should not be underestimated. I know that it is a sensitive subject in the United States, but before the formation and foundation of Israel and the big settlements that were implanted there, there was very little anti-Semitism in the Arab world. Large Jewish communities lived in the Maghreb, North Africa, or in the heart of the Middle East itself in Egypt and Iraq. The Baghdadi Jews in particular were proud of their origins. They regarded themselves as Arab Jews. They were proud of the cuisine they produced, and, of course, their passion for literature and ideas made them susceptible to modernist influences. Many of them were founders of the Egyptian and Iraqi Communist parties. That's how integrated they were in those societies. This was all destroyed by the Zionist project and the creation of Israel. Obviously, the result has been a lot of crude anti-Semitism. But please don't think it comes out of something fundamental to Islam. It does not. In fact, anti-Semitism in the Arab world did not exist in that shape or form until the twentieth century.

So the rage of which Bernard Lewis talks is a different rage from the one I see, because he sees it as inherent in civilizational differences. I see the differences as being fundamentally political and economic. The citizens of these countries say, "It's our oil. We should control it. When nationalist politicians come who want to assert our rights over the oil, in our own interests, you fight wars against them and destroy them." This is what happened with Nasser: two oil wars. The third oil war was fought when Saddam Hussein took Kuwait because he misread signals from the United States. But what he was doing, after all, is now what the United States is doing: effecting a regime change because of a small state that was, without doubt, provoking him. That's all he was doing—this is now acceptable behavior for the United States. But he was punished for doing it. So people see all these wars as oil wars, and now we are seeing another one in Iraq. That's not a civilizational conflict; it's a clash be-tween native people who happen to be Muslims and the world's largest, most powerful empire.

If you read Huntington's book, you will see he has these formulas, which he's now modified in the wake of September 11. In the book he says, We, the West, are a Judeo-Christian civilization. We are now confronted by other civilizations: Islamic civilization and Chinese civilization—he doesn't mention African civilization be-cause, he says, he is not sure such a thing exists. The big danger, according to Huntington, lies in a possible unifi-cation of Chinese and Islamic civilizations. When you read between the lines—and you don't have to read too far between the lines—these are coded messages for the phenomenal growth of the Chinese economy and Chi-nese exports to the United States, and the centrality of Arab oil. That, in my opinion, is what all this civilizational nonsense boils down to.

In my book *The Clash of Fundamentalisms,* I call this a clash between a tiny religious fundamentalism, which is very retrogressive and retrograde, and the mother of all fundamentalisms, American imperial fundamentalism. The American empire, the most powerful in history, now uses its economic and military muscle to reshape the world according to its needs and its interests. Resistance against this is bound to develop. At the moment, it's taken the form of an ultrareligious fundamentalism, which will not succeed because it has nothing to offer. But this will change, and other forms of resistance will emerge. The notion that you can have a large empire that seeks to dominate the world with no resistance at all is laughable.

Talk to the average American listener who is going to hear this broadcast. "Well, Mr. Ali, even though you've said many interesting things, I'm not quite sure. How do I get a better understanding of what the United States is doing and how the world system operates? What suggestions do you have?"

One of the suggestions I would make is, please, don't ignore history. One of the things that has happened in our culture as a whole, not just in the United States but also in Europe and other parts of the world, is that history as a subject has become devalued. If you read the history of the United States, you will find not just the history of an empire in the making, but also the history of dissent in the United States. You will find many surprising things: Walt Whitman, for instance, is supposed to be the poet of liberation, antislavery and pro-Lincoln—and he was, later in his life. But in his earlier years, Whitman was a firm believer in America and the right of American whites as a superior civilization to crush Mexico because it was a lesser civilization—he actually said as much. All of the early American writers and poets felt a certain ambiguity toward American expansionism, but by and large they supported it. This changed by the end of the nineteenth century, with Mark Twain and Whitman. Whitman was deeply shaken by the Civil War, when he realized how much blood had been spilled.

I always say to my American friends that America is a very rich country in every way. It is rich economically. It is rich with the dissenting movements that have grown up within it. And it has committed a wealth of atrocities all over the world. And you have to choose which of these riches you want. Martin Luther King, the year before he was assassinated, said that "the greatest purveyor of violence in the world" was his own country. People should remember that the most gifted and capable American dissenters, many of whom, by the way, were killed by the state, have been people who stood up and resisted, from the Industrial Workers of the World to the African American rebels of the 1960s and 1970s: Joe Hill, Malcolm X, and Martin Luther King Jr.

Many American citizens—not all of them—live comfortably and guzzle gas, and they should understand where this gas comes from. They should think about the people who live in those parts of the world, how American policies affect them, and ask themselves the question, for the sake of their children and grandchildren and the generations to come, "Can we carry on living in a world whose priorities are so upside down?" Because what we are seeing now is a world which is very interlinked and interrelated, and it could all go under by the end of this century unless a serious attempt is made to turn things around.

3

Bush in Babylon

After September 11, a debate began among a number of us who were analyzing why it happened and how to prevent similar acts from happening again. In the early weeks and months, I encountered spokesmen from the Bush administration and the Republican Party in different parts of the world. It was not a very pleasant experience, but it was necessary. We asked them: What do you really want? If your aim is to stop the flow of recruits into organizations like al Qaeda, there is a clear way to accomplish that. If, however, you want to use these events as a pretense to get your way throughout the world, we cannot be of any assistance. It is the latter option, of course, that they took.

Had they decided that the real problem was the despair and bitterness in the Muslim world and the Arab world, and asked themselves, "How are we going to stop

This speech, delivered by Tariq Ali in October 2003, was broadcast on *Alternative Radio*.

the kids from going in the direction they're headed," two issues would have come up immediately. The first one is Palestine, almost a blind spot in America. The second is the campaign of sanctions against Iraq, which had been policed by the United Nations for nearly twelve years, and the weekly bombing raids against Iraq that began soon after the Gulf War, sanctioned by the United Nations. Iraq had been under continuous bombardment for more years than any other country in the world, including during the Second World War. The war in Iraq and the bombing of Iraq went on much longer than the bombing of Vietnam.

To the administration and its apologists here and in Europe, we said, There are two ways. One is to wage more war, which will produce more terrorism, more attacks, and more violence. The other is to devise a political solution to these problems. As far as Iraq is concerned, we urge you to lift the sanctions against Iraq, which have crippled that country and its population, and led to the death of a half a million children from malnourishment according to UNESCO figures. The sanctions made the Iraqi people more dependent than ever on the regime in order to survive, to get health facilities and food subsidies. The sanctions make people more dependent on the regime, not less. You can't have it both ways, claiming this is an evil, vicious dictatorship, while at the same time forcing Iraqis to depend on it.

Furthermore, we urged, the question of Palestine

must be solved. The continuing occupation of Palestine by the Israeli state will never appeal to people in the Muslim and Arab worlds. It will create more bitterness, more despair, and more anger. The Americans and Israelis claim that they offered the Palestinians everything and they refused; no one believes this. Nothing was offered, other than the status of a permanent protectorate. The Oslo accords, as my dear friend the late Edward Said used to say, offered Palestinians nothing. All they offered was shriveled little Bantustans, divided from each other by Israeli roads on which Palestinians are not allowed, infiltrated permanently by Israeli settlers, and continuously patrolled by Israeli tanks. The South African Bantustans had more independence than that. The outbreak of the second intifada, considering this, was hardly a surprise. The intifada was not merely an uprising against Israel and Sharon—it was an uprising against the Palestinian leadership that signed the Oslo accords and then did nothing. The Americans, needless to say, did not heed this advice. And then Ariel Sharon became a valued ally in the war against terrorism.

Vladimir Putin of Russia also became a valued ally in the war against terrorism. He has killed more Chechens than Milosevic killed Kosovars. The city of Grozny was razed to the dust. But that was fine, because Putin was "fighting terrorism."

The world sits and watches, a world where human rights has become a code word for doing whatever needs to be done to occupy countries. But as far as Palestine is concerned, the Western world—and especially the United States—is blind.

There is more criticism of Sharon's actions in the Israeli press than in the American media. When I meet people from the *Washington Post* or the *New York Times*, I ask them why they don't just reprint a few reports each week from the Israeli media. These are Israelis leveling these criticisms. The reports are written in Hebrew; just print them in English.

Before Sharon went into the Occupied Territories, an Israeli colonel was quoted in the Israeli newspaper *Maariv* as follows: "If the politicians send us in to occupy the Palestinian territories, whether people like it or not, the tactics we will have to use in repressing them will be the same tactics as were used by the Germans in occupying the Warsaw ghetto." This is an Israeli colonel speaking, not a Palestinian. It was reported in the Israeli press, on the Internet, and on dissident Web sites. In the *New York Times*? The *Washington Post*? Forget about it. Even the European papers, who cover this issue much better, did not report it.

There was an amazing intervention by one of the Zionist leaders of Israel, the former speaker of Israel's parliament, the Knesset, Avraham Burg, who wrote a moving cry to his own countrymen, saying: What have we become? Do you realize what we are doing to the Palestinians? Have you forgotten what we have suffered ourselves? Don't you realize that if you reduce them to this degree of bitterness and anger and leave them nothing, they have no option but to do what they are doing? Do you think this will end well? He wrote, "I am ashamed to be a Zionist because our philosophy was not to do this to other people but to get a homeland for ourselves." This article was printed in the Israeli press, and then reprinted in every single leading European newspaper. It had a massive impact in Europe. But Burg spoke out because he realized the situation was untenable—it couldn't carry on like that. If you keep oppressing a people, if you reduce them to a level where it's almost easier to die than to live, people do desperate things. They do desperate things not because they want to, but because they feel there is no other channel left.

In the wake of September 11, the Americans missed an opportunity to settle the Palestinian question by pressuring the Israelis to pull back to the 1967 borders and grant the Palestinians a sovereign, independent, democratic republic. This was a big mistake, and they are paying the price for it. That one act alone would have diminished, for many young people in the Arab world, the attraction of groups like al Qaeda. But Washington did not follow that route; instead, it backed Ariel Sharon.

One day, after September 11, according to Bob Woodward, there was a meeting at the White House of the National Security Council. The intellectual giants sitting around the table—George Bush, Dick Cheney, John

Ashcroft, Condi Rice, and others—were embroiled in a heated debate: Should America attack Afghanistan or Iraq? Iraq had absolutely nothing to do with September 11—absolutely nothing. The al Qaeda leadership hated the Iraqi regime because it was totally secular; there were big clashes between al Qaeda supporters and the Ba'athists, both in Syria and in Iraq. If Woodward is to be believed and he talked to all the top official sources, Condi Rice was saying, right after September 11, Let's use 9/11 to get our own way everywhere in the world.

In the end, they went into Afghanistan, which we don't hear very much about these days. It's not in the papers or on our television screens, but it is a total and complete mess. Hamid Karzai, the puppet leader put into power, does little more than wear his lovely shawls about—I'm sure he would much rather be modeling them in Paris or New York than running Afghanistan, where he is so confident of his popularity that his entourage is composed entirely of U.S. Marines. Karzai can't do anything—Afghanistan is run by the Northern Alliance—and he admits that he is powerless. Karzai's older brother runs an Afghan restaurant in Baltimore; at least he's doing something useful—he's feeding a few people. But not Hamid. I like to tell his friends in the U.S. administration and the British foreign office that if they really like him, they should pull him out of the country—they've only shortened his life span by sending him there; he won't last long.

The Taliban, which we were told was the most evil force in the world, are now negotiating behind the scenes because they don't trust the Northern Alliance. I would not be surprised to see, within the next year, a new coalition government in Kabul which includes a large chunk of the former Taliban. Discussions are already taking place.

Then we have Iraq. What was the point of this war—the oil? I don't think so. America needs the oil, of course, but that's why the entire region is swamped with billions of dollars worth of security arrangements. Had it been merely for the oil, however, the Americans could have just made a deal with the regime—as they did in the 1980s, when Hussein was at his worst. So it was not just the oil. It was a display of imperial power; not just for the Arab world, and not just to appease the Israelis—who wanted Hussein removed at all costs because he was backing the Palestinians and he seemed a potential future threat. It was a display of imperial power for all their potential rivals in the Far East and in Europe—to say, We can do it.

Think about the nuclear bombs dropped on Hiroshima and Nagasaki—attacking civilians with weapons of mass destruction. Why did the United States drop not one but two atomic bombs? Not because they were about to be defeated; indeed, Japan was on the edge of collapse. These bombs were a shot across the bow of the Soviets—still an ally, but shortly to become a rival—to say, We can do it. We've got the bombs and you do not.

The occupation of Iraq was a demonstration of military might, for the benefit of America's rivals around the world: We have the power to do this and you do not. It was a warning to the Chinese, the Koreans, and the Japanese: Don't tangle with us.

I warned them before the war began that the occupation of Iraq would not look like Kosovo. This is an independent Arab country, a young country, formed in the 1920s, that resisted the British Empire during three decades of occupation. Every single year there was a rebellion against the British in some part of Iraq. I tried to tell the Americans: Many Iraqis may hate Saddam Hussein, but they will hate you even more.

The Americans did not believe us; they believed the quislings and the collaborators—some were on their payroll and others wanted to be. Kanan Makiya, Fouad Ajami, and their hangers-on went to the White House and told the Americans their troops would be welcomed with "sweets and flowers" in Iraq, according to the *New York Times*.

The troops, of course, were met with hostility everywhere they went, and this critically damaged the morale of the American soldiers, who had been given two contradictory instructions. In the first, Iraq was a barbaric country led by evil ragheads—just pure racism. In the second, the Iraqi people were waiting to be liberated. These contradictory missions were never articulated together, but both were frequently invoked.

The soldiers naturally preferred the second of these missions. They wanted to believe they were going to liberate a country which was dying and crying to be free; but when they arrived, they found a hostile population. Yesterday's *New York Times* described a soldier, back on furlough, who said, "What shook us was the anger and the hostility—the way people looked at us. We had no business being in that country," he said. These soldiers, unfortunately, are realizing this the hard way.

I am surprised to find a large number of Americans and Britons who cannot understand that the Iraqi people do not like being occupied by the United States—it was not something the Iraqis dreamt about. No one understood this until they occupied the country, and now they are in a mess.

Had there been no Iraqi resistance—if the Americans arrived amid silence, even a sullen silence—this war would be seen as a massive triumph, and all those who were even marginally critical would have been silenced. Instead, the resistance in Iraq has given courage to a few Democratic politicians to speak up against the war. They're all jostling around, because most of them supported it—they're claiming they always had their doubts. Why didn't we hear these doubts at the time, when there were lopsided votes for war in Congress? The resistance was necessary to raise doubts, just as the resistance in Vietnam and the struggle there lifted the peace movement in this country to new heights. There is a dialectical relationship at work—resistance abroad, opposition at home—and we can see this in Iraq today.

The Americans are desperately trying to crush the resistance; they have acquired a fig leaf of support from the United Nations, so they can trumpet the UN's backing. This in a region where the UN is hated for its role in the sanctions regime. Bringing blue-helmeted mercenaries into Iraq is no better than having Poles, Ukrainians, or Bulgarians there. These Eastern European countries, who were once called "satellite countries" because they did whatever the Soviet Union wanted, remain satellite countries—now they do just what the United States wants. Old habits die hard, especially when the men in charge of these countries are virtually the same—they've just changed their coats.

Today's colonialism takes place in the age of neoliberal economics, but don't think for a moment that neoliberal policy can deliver goods in Afghanistan and Iraq that it is incapable of providing at home. These are people who are privatizing everything in their home countries, attacking public provisions in education and in health care—how will they create a health service or an education system in Afghanistan and Iraq? After the Second World War, the Americans only pushed forward the Marshall Plan because they faced a serious rival—the Soviet Union. Revolutions were erupting all over the world, in China, Vietnam, Indonesia, and later in Cuba. They needed to put reforms in place to make the system more attractive, but now America has no rival—all that counts is money and profits.

Money and profits, in this age of the Washington consensus, do not give the people of Iraq or Afghanistan what they need or what they desire. The reconstruction of Iraq being discussed would be contracted almost entirely to American firms; the French and the Germans object because they want their own companies in competition— that's the big difference between the two sides. In the Middle East, this war appears to be between the North and the South—with different factions in the North fighting over their share of the loot.

In my book *Bush in Babylon,* I explain why the British occupation of Iraq failed after three decades—they had thirty years and couldn't make it work. A British intelligence team went to conduct a study in Iraq in the 1940s and concluded the British had created "an oligarchy of racketeers" in Iraq. In the 1940s, when there was more of an interest in creating a different sort of world, this was the best they could do. In the world of today, Iraq has something even worse than an oligarchy of racketeers— an oligarchy of foreign racketeers.

The British created racketeers and landlords to establish a social base for themselves in that country, but the United States is taking everyone from outside because they don't trust the Iraqis. Even the people cleaning up the U.S. barracks are South Asian or Filipino immigrants. How can they ever expect the people of Iraq to trust them?

It was amazing to see Paul Wolfowitz in Baghdad, addressing a press conference composed mainly of Western journalists, telling them, "I think all foreigners should stop interfering in the internal affairs of Iraq." He's referring to other Arabs, of course, but these people are so unself-conscious it's becoming difficult to satirize them. You have one-third of the British army and tens of thousands of American soldiers, who have come thousands of miles to occupy an Arab country—and this idiot stands up and says the problem is there are too many foreigners.

What you are not told by the mainstream media in this country is that a large chunk of the Iraqi population is hostile to the occupation; they don't want it. Were a free election to take place, by some miracle, the first two demands of the new parliament would be to eject all occupation troops and seize back control of Iraq's oil. What would the Americans do then? They would be forced to do what they did in Iran in 1953, when they toppled the democratically elected government of Mohammed Mossadegh after he nationalized Anglo-Iranian oil—another regime change. They do not like oil-producing countries to be governed by democratic regimes, because there's always a risk.

Look at the attempts to remove Chavez from power in Venezuela, after he had been elected six times in different ways by the population. Even its enemies admit the Venezuelan constitution is the most democratic constitution in Latin America; it was pushed through by Chavez against the will of the oligarchy and backed by two-thirds of the population in a referendum. The Americans don't have the excuse they used in Iraq—that it's not democratic. Why did they try to overthrow it? Why did they back the oligarchy? Why are the generals who are trying to topple Chavez on your payroll?

Chavez was deposed, arrested, and locked up for forty-eight hours, but there was a mass rebellion. All the poor people in Caracas from the slums came out onto the streets: half a million people marched onto the Mira Flores Palace, demanding to know where Chavez had been taken. And then an amazing thing happened: the general who had carried out the coup inadvertently set off a mutiny in the army. As the president of the chamber of commerce—a well-known crook, the Venezuelan equivalent of Ahmed Chalabi—was being sworn in as the new president of Venezuela, this general told the army band, "Play the national anthem when the new president comes out—the television cameras will be here." The soldiers in the band refused: Chavez is our elected president, they protested. The general turned to the bugler, a seventeen-year-old, and demanded that he play the trumpet to honor the president. But this kid says to the general, We elected Chavez; he is our president. The general says, You will follow my orders—I'm a general. And the bugler just says, Play it yourself if you're so keen to greet the new president.

What gives a young soldier that confidence? He feels empowered by his government, which is trying to do nothing too radical—just to use the oil money to improve the conditions of the poor, give them more schools, more health, more education, more shelter. A traditional Roosevelt-era New Deal program, and that's all. The United States tried to topple Chavez because the example might spread.

If you read the *New York Times,* you know what's going on in Bolivia—a massive insurrection against another rogue president, this one backed by the United States. Seventy people have been shot dead. The poorest of the poor in Bolivia are being shot dead, and the State Department is backing their killers.

When the empire behaves in this way, all the while claiming that they act in the interest of democracy and freedom, I tend to doubt it. Forgive me. The record tells us something very different—all they do is for their own interests, and this has always been true, whether we are talking about the American empire or the British one.

The Romans used to make similar arguments. In his essay on Agricola, the most prominent Roman proconsul in Britain, the Roman historian Tacitus describes a very telling incident, when Agricola stood at the shore of Britain, looked across the sea to Ireland, and asked what it was. You don't even need to look in that direction, his ad-

visers replied; it is a useless place of bog lands and primi-
tive tribesmen, so remote from civilization it has nothing
to offer our great empire. But that's not the point, Agricola said. Is it occupied by Roman legions or not? It is
not, the advisers said. That, Agricola announced, is where
the danger lies, because people here in Britain will say, If
that island is not occupied by Roman legions, perhaps
one day we too will be free.

This also helps to explain the occupation of Iraq and
the continuing attacks on Syria—the two Arab countries
which still refuse to toe the American line, to become essentially subordinate states in that region and accept Israeli hegemony.

The final argument of the empire—not the politicians so much as the tame intellectuals, the pundits, and
the press—when they attack the Arab world, is one of
cultural difference. We are very different from the Arab
world, they say. The Arabs are incapable of being critical
of themselves. The Arabs blame everything on the United
States. I've read this argument in the Western press quite
often, but it is simply not true. In fact, if you travel
around the Arab world, you can go into any tea house or
any café, in any Arab capital, and you will hear some of
the most vicious and savage criticism of the Arab regimes.
This is a much more politically conscious population than
that of the United States of America—that may be a cultural difference. Everyone is engaged. They want to know
how to change these wretched people who rule them,

and their hostility to the United States derives, often, from the fact that many of these regimes exist only because of American backing and support.

The intellectuals and poets who have spoken out are incredibly self-critical; it is very common in the Arab world, where it is hardly the case that people blame the United States for no reason. They blame the United States because it sustained odious regimes in Egypt, in Saudi Arabia, in the Gulf states, and for a long time in Iraq, and it does to this day. The United States is seen not as an advocate of democracy, but rather its opposite.

The Iraqi poets who have been exiled by Saddam Hussein are totally opposed to the occupation. When I met with the great Arab poet Saadi Youssef, the day after Baghdad fell, he was crying. He said to me, There were three great poets in Iraq: me, [Mohammed Mahdi] al-Jawahri, and Mudhaffar al-Nawab. Al-Jawahri died at the age of 100. Saddam used to send us messenger after messenger, saying, "I know you're radicals, I know you hate me, but you are part of the heritage of Iraq; come and recite at a poetry reading in Baghdad and there will be a million people." He was right   there would've been a million people to listen to these three great poets. "We never went," Saadi Youssef said. "Too many of our comrades had been killed when the CIA gave Saddam the lists of communists to wipe out. He did it for them. That hurt. Mudhaffar al-Nawab, my comrade in exile, said Saddam might kill us, the son of a bitch. We don't trust him. We told his ambassador, We don't want to come. The ambassador said, 'Saddam says the blood on his neck guarantees your safety.' Somehow this was not very reassuring."

One month before the invasion of Iraq, all of these exiles who have now been put into power, backed by the CIA and British intelligence, held a secret meeting in a London hotel. Saadi Youssef saw this from his London exile and said, "It's a jackals' wedding."

"In southern Iraq," Youssef continued, "in the summer months when we sleep under the stars in the night to keep cool, once every six months or three months a village will report there was a conclave of jackals. They come, they make a noise, they queue to mate, and there's a stench that is unbearable. The next day the villagers get up and they say, Did you notice that? Did you smell that jackals' wedding? It's forgotten then, because you don't hear from them for some time." He sat down when this conference of collaborators, the so-called Iraqi National Congress, took place in London, and he wrote a wonderful poem called "The Jackals' Wedding," for which he is not permitted to return to Iraq. This poem circulated around the world via the Internet, and ordinary people all over referred to the collaborators as "the jackals' wedding."

> O Mudhaffar al-Nawab,
> my life-long comrade,
> what are we to do about the jackals' wedding?

You remember the old days:
In the cool of the evening
under bamboo roof
propped on soft cushions stuffed with fine wool
we'd sip tea (a tea I've never since tasted)
among friends . . .
Night falls as softly as our words
under the darkening crowns of the date palms
while smoke curls from the hearth, such fragrance
as if the universe had just begun

. . .

Then a cackling explodes
from the long grass and date palms—
the jackals' wedding!

. . .

O, Mudhaffar al-Nawab—
today isn't yesterday
(truth is as evanescent as the dream of a child)—
truth is, this time we're at their wedding reception,
yes, the jackals' wedding
you've read their invitation

. . .

O, Mudhaffar al-Nawab,
let's make a deal:

I'll go in your place
      (Damascus is too far away from that secret hotel [in
      London])

I'll spit in the jackals' faces,
I'll spit on their lists,
I'll declare that we are the people of Iraq—
we are the ancestral trees of this land,
proud beneath our modest roof of bamboo.

This is the spirit of the Iraqi people—who are resisting, who suffered under Saddam but refuse to accept the occupation.

This illustrates how important culture is to the politics of that world and how the two are interrelated, something people in the West seem not to understand. Youssef's poem is addressed to another poet in exile, Mudhaffar al-Nawab, who was locked up by Saddam, sought refuge in Iran, was locked up and tortured by the Shah, and then sent back to Iraq; he has been in exile since the late 1970s. He has long been adored by young Iraqis, and his tapes circulate all over the country. He wrote:

I have accepted my fate
Is like that of a bird,
And I have endured all
Except humiliation,
Or having my heart
Caged in the Sultan's palace.
But dear god
Even birds have homes to return to,
I fly across this homeland

From sea to sea,
And to prison after prison after prison,
Each jailer embracing the other.

How can we resist this empire—this all-powerful empire with no rivals? The Security Council has now caved in, which is no big surprise. The resistance in the occupied lands will carry on as long as the occupation continues. The Americans will have their highs, their ups, their lows, their downs, but it will carry on. An occupied Iraq and an occupied Palestine will never be at peace.

We need a strong dissenting opposition in the heart of the empire, and that is why all of you, the citizens of this empire, are so important. You are responsible, not directly but collectively, for this regime in power— certainly if the choice had been up to the rest of the world, Bush would not be president today.

It is no use to be paranoid about this regime; it can be toppled. It's not all-powerful, but it can only be toppled if there is an opposition. Do you know what is the big difference between Iraq and the United States? In Iraq there is an opposition. Here you have the Democrats, who wriggle, who wiggle, who say one thing one day, one thing the other. You need a tough voice to challenge the lies on every level. I don't believe it can't be done, but it requires politicians with guts, and a real movement.

In this country, many people believe the American empire and American imperialism came into being after

the Russian Revolution; it's not true. This empire has existed for a long time, but it's not a traditional sort of empire, and it became a *world* power after 1917. It doesn't
like colonial occupation—it prefers to rule through reli-
able relays, whether they are oligarchies, military dictatorships, or politicians. Iraq is an exceptional case in this
regard, just as the Philippines were in the last years of the
nineteenth century.

The occupation of the Philippines brought out the
best in American liberalism. Mark Twain and Henry
James and William James and a whole host of intellectuals
put out a call to form an anti-imperialist league to stop
these occupations from taking place. Within two years it
had a quarter of a million members in twenty-five big
American cities. That is what we are lacking. We have an
antiwar movement which goes up and down, but we need
a consistent intellectual offensive against the lies.

There is opposition in this country, and there is
anger, but it has to be mobilized. And if you completely
fall into the trap of "anyone but Bush," there will only be
more problems. I want Bush to be removed, for God's
sake, but it can't be done apolitically. This regime is horri-
ble, but it's no different from many that came before it—
people have short memories. We are angry about the
PATRIOT Act. It's disgusting, of course. But have we forgotten Attorney General Palmer's raids, which locked up
and deported large numbers of German and Italian immigrants? Have we forgotten COINTELPRO, imple-

mented by a Democratic administration during the Vietnam War to spy on members of the antiwar movement? These moves are part and parcel of the empire's self-defense mechanisms, and they are not new—we can't exaggerate the threat they pose. I do not accept the notion that somehow this is qualitatively different from what we've seen in the past.

One positive result of this absurd, irrational war of occupation in Iraq is that a whole generation of young people have become more engaged in politics than the generation that preceded them. On the day that the bombing of Baghdad began, hundreds of thousands of students, both in North America and in Europe, poured out onto the streets, chanting slogans they had made up—the slogans of their own generation, taken from rock and punk songs. In London they chanted, "Who let the bombs out?" It has become cool again to be politically engaged, and this is important.

In this war of the North against the South, of the great empire against future rivals and people it characterizes as its current enemies, nothing is more crucial than a vigorous opposition, here in the heart of the empire itself.

4

Cracks in the Empire

Babylon is one of the great cities of antiquity located in Mesopotamia, along with Nineveh, Ur, and Samarra. Why did you call your book Bush in Babylon?

It just came to me instinctively. When Amy Goodman on *Democracy Now* asked me that same question, I had to devise a quick answer, and this is what I came up with: The only town in Mesopotamia that George Bush might possibly be aware of is Babylon, because it appears in the Old Testament. I thought if by some mischance he came across this book, he would understand the title immediately—that's where he is currently mired. As you know, in the Old Testament Babylon is a wicked town, so there is a double entendre: *Bush in Babylon* also means Bush is stuck in wickedness. I thought born-again Christians might appreciate the title.

This interview, conducted in November 2003, first appeared in *International Socialist Review* (January–February 2004) and was broadcast on *Alternative Radio*.

You begin your book asking: "Why are otherwise intelligent people in Britain and the United States surprised to learn that the occupation is detested by a majority of Iraqi citizens?" Why is that?

I think it's because the United States has never been occupied, at least not as a modern country. The last time the American mainland was hit, apart from September 11, was in the early part of the nineteenth century. So they have no idea what it is to be occupied; the same is true of Britain, which has not been under occupation since the time of the Roman Empire. Citizens in these two countries have no idea what it means to be occupied by a foreign power, whereas a large part of Europe and of the colonial world is all too familiar with occupation. Second, there's an arrogance in the world in which we live that says they should feel lucky to be occupied by the United States. What's wrong with them? Why are they getting so upset? We're doing them a big favor. Third, there is no awareness of Iraqi history in the mainstream media. I'm shocked to find that even in the American intelligence agencies there is a lack of knowledge. If anyone had known the history of Iraq—and certainly the British do, and they should have warned these guys—there is a long history of resisting empires. The last reason is that the networks like FOX News, which dominate people's consciousness, failed to provide an adequate picture of Iraq's history and culture, and what the Americans were going to get into. How can you have an alert and vigilant citizenry with such a high degree of deliberately fostered ignorance?

Talk about what happened in Iraq after the British took over from the Turks at the end of World War I. There was resistance.

There certainly was. People have to understand that the Ottoman Empire, which had many strengths but also many weaknesses, was quite a relaxed empire. As long as the occupied lands sent in money to the central treasury, they were more or less left alone. The Arab world under the Ottomans was not divided. It was a world dominated by cities—Damascus, Cairo, Baghdad, and Jerusalem. These were big Ottoman cities, and populations traveled easily between them. The Ottoman system had provinces, vilayets. The three that divided Iraq were Mosul, Baghdad, and Basra. Turkey made a foolish mistake in the First World War and decided to go with Germany; it is interesting to speculate what would have happened in the Arab world had Turkey gone with the other side. After the war, the Ottoman Empire in the Middle East was divided between the French and the British, and the British, being the dominant empire, got the lion's share; the French got Lebanon and Syria. One can see different patterns: where the British ruled they imposed monarchies because that was their system at home; where the French ruled they established French-dominated republics. So you have different colonial traditions. The British colonial practice in Iraq was to look for a monarch. They looked around, and there were lots of contenders. Finally they picked the Hashemite family in Saudi Arabia—to whom they had promised Syria. They had promised Feisal he could be king of Greater Arabia, but the French said, No way, we don't want a king. So they had to find this poor guy a throne, and they gave him Iraq. He was unhappy from the beginning because he wasn't independent; he knew he was simply an instrument of the British Empire. From then on—while the British governed Iraq through the twenties, thirties, and forties—there was resistance of one sort or another. In fact, the first time chemical weapons were used in the Arab world was during the bombing of Kurdish villages in Iraq by the British Royal Air Force in the late 1920s. There were general strikes in Baghdad, mutinies in the Iraqi army, armed resistance in Mosul and Basra. All this has already happened once before.

Eat the State, *a radical, antiauthoritarian journal from Seattle, quotes a U.S. army colonel who says, "It was a big mistake to discount the Iraqi resistance. If someone invaded Texas, we'd do the same thing."*

I've been arguing since the beginning of the occupation of Iraq that the people who know the most about what is really going on are the American soldiers and officers, because they see the reality every day. The media can lie to citizens in the United States, but it can't lie to soldiers in the field because they know what's going on. I read on the Internet there is a woman—a Lieutenant Colonel Karen Kwiatkowski—who worked as a policy analyst for the Pentagon but is now horrified about what is going on in Iraq and Palestine. She said what our country is doing in this region is monstrous. I think it would be a strange irony, but a fitting one, if the true picture of what's happening in Iraq is finally transmitted back into the U.S. by the soldiers, or the families of soldiers killed, or those who come back without arms or legs. These are the people who will begin to tell the truth to their communities in a much, much bigger way than people like us ever could.

Bechtel, which won the contract to privatize Bolivia's water, was also one of the big winners of the Iraq war—it's gotten huge contracts. So there have been some winners in Iraq— Halliburton, Bechtel, Lockheed Martin, Northrop Grumman. There are profits to be made from imperial aggression.

There certainly are profits to be made, though I wonder if they will be as high as the corporations imagine. In order to start the reconstruction you have invest a large amount of money—for security guards and mercenaries who have to be paid. If the Iraqi resistance continues with its scorched-earth tactics, a lot of these cities could be blown up again, and I think some of these corporations are aware of this. They had to be bullied and pushed to go in there, because they knew the security situation was not good. It seems possible they will get their comeuppance in Iraq.

One of the striking features of Bush in Babylon *is the use of poetry. You grew up with the poetry of Faiz Ahmed Faiz, Muhammad Iqbal, and others. In your book you cite such Arab poets as Nizar Qabbani, Saadi Youssef, and Mudhaffar al-Nawab. Why did you introduce poetry in what is a very political book?*

Because Arab culture in the broader sense—including political culture—is dominated by poetry, and people in the West are simply not aware of this. Poetry plays a very important role in the culture. It's not an elite thing at all, as it has become in the West. Poetry readings here in England are attended by fifty to two hundred people, at most. In the Arab world and the Muslim world, you have poetry readings attended by tens of thousands. When I was growing up in Pakistan, I would go to poetry readings that would start after dinner, about 10:30 P.M., and still be under way when it came time for breakfast. By the morning, we were just swaying with the rhythm of the words—a chant would go up from the crowd to recite some extemporary poetry, make it up. The poets would then have a competition: they would decide on a subject and recite poetry, and the audience would judge who was the best.

There is one story that is linked in a strange way to empire. The United States prefers ruling Pakistan through the military. When it carried out its first coup in 1958, the great Punjabi poet Ustad Daman, who was an oral poet (his poetry is only written down occasionally) gave a big poetry reading. Some of our best poets were in prison, and Ustad Daman came to recite. He was a big man with a wonderful voice, and recited some apolitical poems about birds fluttering here and there. And we said, "Birds flutter anywhere; say something about today." He carried on, but we pressed him, and he got angry and recited a poem extemporaneously. The poem, in Punjabi, went something like this: "Now each day is fair and balmy. Everywhere you look: the army." This poem got him imprisoned. He was picked up the next day and locked up for three weeks. The next time he met us, he said, "Come here you mothers. Don't you ever tell me at a poetry reading to say something, because I go to prison and not you guys." This was the tradition I grew up in, and it's a tradition that is also very strong in the Arab world. It is a tradition where a poem written by Nizar Qabbani, the fine Syrian poet, or Mahmoud Darwish, the national poet of Palestine, is immediately picked up by ordinary people in cafés, and crosses frontiers without any problems. The great singers of the Arab world then sing these poems. When Oum Kalsoum sings Qabbani or another poet, that poem is transformed; it's heard by millions. As a result, people sing it or recite it, and these poets become like cult figures. In countries where politicians are by and large venal, and do not represent what people want, the poets have become the conscience of the world. People in the West say: The Arabs don't have a critical culture; they always blame the West. That's rubbish, as you will see if you read the poetry of the Arab world. Nizar Qabbani is more critical of the Arab leaders than anyone else. They express this anger with their own leadership, and this has earned them the respect of the populace. The people know that the poets are good, that they speak for us, and they can't be bought.

Much has happened since our last meeting a year ago at the World Social Forum in January 2003. I want to ask you about the massive outpouring on February 15. You were involved in the London demonstration against the projected U.S. attack on Iraq. Were you surprised at the turnout?

I was very surprised. We were expecting about 200,000 people in London. We thought if we were lucky it might reach 250,000, which would have been tremendous—one of the largest demonstrations ever in Britain. When I arrived at the demonstration I was just stunned—the crowd was unending. The police, for once, were very friendly; senior police chiefs came up to me and said, You must be very proud today. I asked them for their estimates—this was just at the beginning of the demonstration—and they said people are still pouring in, but our official sources are saying half a million people on the streets already. By the time the demonstration reached Hyde Park we had a million and a half people in London. It was the biggest demonstration in the history of Britain. We had never seen anything like it.

The makeup of this demonstration was interesting. The overwhelming bulk of those who came were not people from the Left; not radicals; not people who had any link with progressive causes. This was the most moving part of it. These were ordinary citizens, who did not believe the lies of their politicians, and who said, We want to stop this war. It was also touching that they actually thought they could stop the war by coming out in large numbers, and in a perfect world, they should have been able to. I spoke at that demonstration, and I said, I'm afraid the war won't stop unless there is regime change in Britain—we need to get rid of this servile government that is permanently stationed at the posterior of the White House whether the occupant is Clinton or Bush. Unless we get rid of governments like this, they will go and make wars. We also predicted that there would be resistance in Iraq. People all over Europe and the United

States genuinely felt they could stop the war, but they didn't realize that the decision to go to war had been made weeks earlier.

Two days after the February 15 demonstrations, the New York Times *said in a front-page story that a new superpower had emerged:"world public opinion." What do you think about that?*

It sounds good. It flatters the demonstrators, but it's not true. Pubic opinion is only public opinion. It has no way to enforce its will. That will only happen if this public opinion has an impact on official politics, but in the U.S., at least, it had zero impact—it did not even register with Democratic politicians. The Democrats ignored the public and went along with Bush: with very few exceptions, they all voted for the war, and basically gave Bush a blank check to do what he wanted. In Britain the demonstrations did have some limited impact. The scale of the protest was such that a considerable number of Labor members of parliament became nervous that they might not get reelected, and challenged Blair in parliament. Blair then lied through his teeth to save himself, insisting that Iraq possessed weapons of mass destruction, which could be deployed to strike Britain on forty-five minutes' notice. He managed to win over some MPs, but if the opposition within the Labor Party had been fifteen or twenty members larger, Blair would have lost and he would have been dependent on Conservative Party votes, which would have been very fitting. He was on the verge of losing the support of his own party—that's why his lies reached such an amazing magnitude.

What do you say to people who marched, protested, sent e-mails, and wrote letters before the war, but now feel, "We've done our best. We couldn't stop it. Game over. I'm going home"?

Well, the game isn't over, and they've got to understand that. I think for many people, this was their first time at a demonstration, and they thought once Iraq was invaded, the game was up. But as we are seeing, the game continues: we now have an Iraqi resistance, which grows every day; the U.S. generals know that they are partially trapped, and they are searching for a way out. In this situation, the big antiwar movements that emerged in February must be revived to lay siege to their congressmen, their senators, and their members of parliament, and say: "We warned you. We told you not to make war, but you went ahead. Now it's our people who are being killed, it's Iraqis who are being killed, it's time to stop it." If they begin to put the pressure on, not just with big demonstrations on the streets, but by addressing complaints to specific congressmen and senators, there could be some effect. The large volume of angry mail congressmen began to receive as the Vietnam War escalated had a real effect on them. We need a repeat of Senator Fulbright's hearings before the Senate Foreign Relations Committee. I remember those hearings—they were shown all over the world. Every night on the BBC, Fulbright would come on, and we could see how he made the administration squirm. Unfortunately, we have very few senators with that kind of integrity at the moment.

Howard Zinn closes his classic A People's History of the United States *with the words of the poet Shelley:*

"Rise like Lions after slumber
In unvanquishable number,
Shake your chains to earth like dew
Which in sleep had fallen on you—
Ye are many—they are few."

That is a great poem, and it demonstrates that the tradition of radical poetry is not confined to the Arab or the Islamic world. It was a very strong strain in nineteenth-century Britain and the United States, and it would be great if it could be revived, if many more of our poets in the West began to intervene, to engage with the world in which we live. Shelley's message is absolutely true, and it illuminates a very interesting lesson from Iraq. The United States is the world's only superpower, the world's only empire, with military superiority on a scale even science-fiction writers could not have dreamt; they can destroy whole countries just by pushing two or three buttons. But when you occupy those countries with your own troops, all that technology is irrelevant: you have to confront a sullen and embittered population, which is what American soldiers are now fighting. Then cracks begin to appear in the empire that once seemed invincible. You begin to realize that when it comes to people, you aren't that strong after all, because they refuse to accept what you are imposing on them. This is how resistance begins, and this resistance shapes the consciousness of the occupied and that of the occupiers and their countrymen as well. Occupying empires perpetually provoke resistance, and eventually this resistance has an impact inside the empire itself. This is the history of all empires, and the United States is not immune from it.

Much of the polite discussion in the United States is really focusing on this particular issue: "They Botched the Occupation." There was a recent New York Times Magazine *cover story by David Rieff, titled "Blueprint for a Mess," rehearsing this argument. Very few people are talking about the illegality or immorality of attacking an independent state that was no threat.*

This is also the position of General Wesley Clark, who says that the problem with the occupation is not that it happened but the way it was done—of course, he thinks he would have done it much better. This is where these people are completely wrong: they believed they could repeat the Balkan experience in the Arab world.

Even if the United Nations had sanctioned the occupation from the start, even if French and German troops fought alongside the British and Americans, the result would have been exactly the same, except that the casualties would have been shared. I don't think it would have been any different. If you sent in blue-helmeted UN troops, the reaction would have been just as hostile, if not more so, because the UN is hated in Iraq for its role in administering the sanctions and permitting the Americans and British to bomb Iraq every week for twelve years. There's no way out of it. What's wrong is the occupation, not the way in which it's being carried out.

In Bush in Babylon *you call the resistance "the Maquis," which conjures up images of brave Frenchmen fighting the Nazi occupiers in the 1940s. There's been a bit of controversy at the* Los Angeles Times *about the term "resistance."*

The management of the *Los Angeles Times* has asked their journalists not to refer to the Iraqi resistance as "the resistance." They would prefer to use words like insurgents, guerrillas, or even terrorists. This isn't going to work—they can change the name as much as they like. I noticed that Christopher Hitchens put the word resistance in scare quotes in a recent *Los Angeles Times* book review. But you can't fool people forever; what is emerging in Iraq is a classic resistance. And it is developing much more quickly than it did in France. In Nazi-occupied

France, the resistance took a long time to get cracking. The American OSS [the predecessor to the CIA] and the British intelligence agencies helped train the resistance; they taught them how to blow up rail lines, kill occupying officers, throw hand grenades, and so on. They were never called terrorists. They were called the Maquis, the Resistance. There was another critical difference in France: a sizeable section of the old establishment collaborated with the Germans—the Vichy regime was not a tiny minority. The puppet regime in Iraq was installed from the outside: Ahmed Chalabi was brought in from the United States, which hired two hundred mercenaries for him and implanted them in Baghdad. And he thinks he's going to be popular. In France, there was at least some portion of the local population that was happy to be occupied by the Germans; in Iraq that's not the case. Very few people—even those most hostile to Saddam—want to be occupied by the United States and Britain. A classic resistance is taking shape, similar to those in Algeria, Vietnam, and parts of Africa. This is how it starts.

Edward Said, the noted Palestinian American professor and author, passed away in September. In one of his essays he wrote "a deep gulf separates Arab culture and civilization from the United States. . . . The notion of an Arab people with traditions, cultures and identities of their own is simply inadmissible in the United States. Arabs are dehumanized, they are seen as violent, irrational terrorists always on the lookout for murder and bomb-

ing outrages. . . . This morbid, obsessional fear and hatred of the Arabs has been a constant theme in U.S. foreign policy since World War Two."

It's also the case that the United States—quite cynically—used the Islamist organizations, at the same time, to fight their other enemies: communism and the secular nationalist regimes. Edward's political sensibility was formed by the 1967 war; prior to that, as he's said, he wasn't engaged. The 1967 war changed his life—it established the Arab world and Palestine as central concerns for him. That war was decisive because the U.S. used Israel as their enforcer to remove the nationalist regimes in Egypt and Syria. The defeat inflicted on these countries marked the death knell of Arab nationalism, which had already peaked: It tried to unite the Arab world but failed.

I remember a time in the late 1950s when you had Radio Baghdad, Radio Cairo, and Radio Damascus inciting Arab citizens to revolt against the pro-Western monarchies, with the result that there was even an attempt at a nationalist coup in Saudi Arabia, from within the Saudi army. The nationalists had to be taught a lesson, and the Israelis were used to teach it. The propaganda that construes the Arab world as one monolithic entity is self-serving. This was never the case; there were always divisions. After the Americans helped the enemies of light destroy all the secular movements in the Arab world, they now have the nerve to complain that the only real opposition in the Arab world is Islamist. The basis for this was laid by the U.S., which wiped out the alternatives. Today, the Islamists are the only ones that oppose the American empire. Secularists were demoralized or intimidated or physically exterminated, and then the NGOs bought off many of the best people with the tacit understanding that they could not engage directly in politics if they wanted to receive funding or assistance.

Unfortunately, the NGOs have helped remove secular intellectuals from politics—their impact on intellectual life in the Muslim world needs to be tabulated. In Pakistan, for example, two Islamist parties won recent elections in key provinces bordering Afghanistan, where in prior elections, they had captured no more than five or six percent of the vote. One of the Islamist leaders spoke openly about how this was possible: the other parties, he said, left us a clean field. We didn't use religion. We didn't say we were going to impose Islamic law. We didn't do anything but attack the American empire. No one else was doing it. That won us the elections.

Afghanistan has somewhat dropped off the radar screen with the focus on Iraq, but there is a lot happening there. There has been a surge of Taliban activity. A New York Times editorial says that Afghanistan is "in danger of reverting to a deadly combination of rule by warlords and the Taliban." What's going on in Afghanistan?

It's very simple. Basically, the United States made a deal with the warlords of the Northern Alliance. They didn't have to fight, and the Taliban melted away. As I said at the time, the Taliban was not going to fight; the faction with Osama would disappear and the faction controlled by Pakistan would be withdrawn. That's what happened. The war was delayed for two or three weeks to allow the Pakistani army to pull its soldiers out of Afghanistan along with as many Taliban fighters as they could. This notion that the Taliban was a totally independent force was not true. Without the support of the Pakistani army, they could never have taken Kabul in the 1990s.

In May 2003, I gave the Eqbal Ahmad Lecture in Islamabad, and I taunted many of the generals there in civilian clothes: The only victory you have won in your entire existence, I said, apart from those against your own people, was taking Kabul. This was your biggest victory, but now you've rolled over like spaniels and unraveled your only military victory. After that a high senior civil servant followed me to Karachi and told me that he carried a message from high up: "Tell him we've only unraveled the victory temporarily. We'll be back, and this time we might go in without beards just to keep the Americans happy." There's a great deal of cynicism inside the Pakistani army.

A very interesting situation has developed in Afghanistan. The Americans installed Hamid Karzai, who worked for U.S. intelligence agencies. He is so popular that he refuses to be guarded by a single Afghan: his entire bodyguard consists of U.S. Marines. His only distinguishing feature is the beautiful shawls that he wears. He's not long for this world if he remains in Afghanistan—the guy has absolutely no legitimacy. The rest of Afghanistan, outside of Kabul, is run by the Northern Alliance and various factions. One faction of the Taliban is gearing up for attacks, while another is basically ready to make a deal with Karzai. That wing, controlled by the Pakistani military, is engaged in secret talks with Zalmay Khalilzad, the American proconsul in Afghanistan. The Americans are attempting to work with this faction of the Taliban and isolate the Northern Alliance. It's back to square one.

Do you remember the beginning of the Afghan war, when Laura Bush and Cherie Blair talked about liberating the women of Afghanistan? This was a new idea to me— the first imperial intervention for women's liberation. But in the end, all it amounted to was a few pictures of one female announcer on Afghan television; she has long since disappeared, and the condition of women is as bad as ever, while incidents of rape have gone up. Only one thing has changed: Prior to the occupation, the heroin trade was dominated by the Taliban and the Northern Alliance—the Taliban heroin went through Pakistan, and the Northern Alliance sent theirs through Central Asia via the Russian Mafia to Kosovo, where it was distributed. Now the Northern Alliance has a complete monopoly on heroin, and various Pakistani entities—including the colonels and generals who were on the take—are suffering quite badly as a result.

In a debate I had with Bill Rammell, one of Blair's MPs, he jettisoned all the reasons that were used to justify the war in Iraq, and he fell back on two arguments: Anyone criticizing the war was anti-American, and aren't the Iraqis better off? Isn't the world a better place with Saddam gone? How would you respond to those arguments?

The anti-American argument suggests that America is a monolith, but we know there is a long history of Americans who have opposed American imperialism. Many others stood up against the depredations of empire by forming the Anti-Imperialist League during the occupation of the Philippines; there is obviously a long tradition of dissent within the United States. The second argument is rubbish. How is the world a better place with an Arab country under occupation, with a war going on—a dual occupation of the Middle East? The world is not a better place; it's a more dangerous place, because this war encourages terrorism. As for Saddam: when his repression was at its worst, he had an audience with Donald Rumsfeld, Reagan's special envoy, who came to visit Baghdad in December 1983. Britain and the United States backed Saddam when he was committing his worst atrocities, during the war with Iran, when he carried out his chemical attacks against the Kurds in 1988. The Left protested these atrocities, but our governments continued to back Saddam. There is no basis for the Americans to claim things are better. It is always preferable for dictators—or the Iranian clerics—to be removed by their own people; then the change remains organic. To be removed by outside forces has given Saddam new life: his popularity is rising; he didn't flee. Iraqis may dislike him a great deal, but many do respect him now.

There's a quote in your book that is appropriate for today: "Next the statesman will invent cheap lies, putting the blame upon the nation that is attacked, and every man will be glad of those conscience-soothing falsities, and will diligently study them, and refuse to examine any refutations of them; and thus he will by and by convince himself that the war is just, and will thank God for the better sleep he enjoys after this process of grotesque self-deception." Who wrote that?

Those wonderful words were written by Mark Twain at the founding of the Anti-Imperialist League; they were published posthumously in *Harper's* magazine in 1916. I think if the Anti-Imperialist League were revived it could garner support in a very broad, nonsectarian way. It shouldn't be restricted to the Left, but draw in a whole range of people. It could take off globally and be a big step forward.

Arundhati Roy writes in War Talk, *"Our strategy should not be only to confront Empire but to lay siege to it. To deprive it of oxygen." How do you deprive an empire of oxygen?*

We shouldn't underestimate the scale of the challenge that confronts us. This is the first time in history that the world has only one empire, and it's not easy to combat. It cannot be defeated militarily. It can be harried and worn down—laid siege to—but a very important part of that effort has come from inside the United States. It has to be a democratic siege. I travel a lot in the United States, and many people come to my talks just for the information. In Minneapolis a guy came up to me and asked, "Is it true Israel has nuclear and chemical weapons?" He asked me, "Why doesn't our president tell us this?" This is a question you're not suppose to raise. I'm constantly amazed at the paucity of information available in the United States.

In Bush in Babylon *you cite Antonio Gramsci, the Italian theorist most feared by the Fascists, who says, "The 'normal' exercise of hegemony is characterized by the combination of force and consent, in variable equilibrium, without force predominating too much over consent." Why does Gramsci attract your attention?*

Because he was the theorist who thought about how capitalism rules the world—in contrast to other theorists, who insisted it was all done through force. If control was established only by force, it would be impossible to maintain indefinitely. Consent by the ruled is crucial to keeping the system alive; this may seem more evident now, but when Gramsci suggested this in the 1920s, it was a hotly debated issue.

Throughout the British Empire's rule in India—apart from the Second World War—there were never more than 36,000 British soldiers in India. How could they control the entire subcontinent with such a small force? They could only do it because they had the support of the ruling elites in India. Once that support began to evaporate, it was possible to end British rule. That's why the British never educated anyone in India—they knew if they educated the bulk of the population it would have been curtains much earlier. When the British left India, it was 85 percent rural and 90 percent illiterate. Gramsci helped me to understand how this kind of consent of the ruled was established. The United States has employed these tactics as well, in Latin America, for example.

Another of Gramsci's insights is also very relevant today: when neither force nor consent is effective, the use of money often comes into play; people can simply be bought off. If you look at the passage of resolutions in the Security Council, you can often see a mixture of the carrot and the stick. States are promised aid if they cast their votes the right way; that's how Israel was accepted in 1948.

Gramsci, who was persecuted and jailed during Mussolini's reign in Italy, talked about cracks in the system—that the opposition needed to use them and point their energy at them because the system wasn't monolithic. In the United States, or in Europe, there are openings. Michael Moore, for example, is very skillful at exploiting them.

There are three fissures in the empire at the moment. The biggest is in Latin America. This is a part of the world dominated by the United States since the proclamation of the Monroe Doctrine. The Marine general Smedley Butler's book on this subject, *War Is a Racket,* is absolutely cracking—he describes how the U.S. Marine Corps was used as a Mafia-style enforcer for the corporations in capturing Central America. This is a book written by a general who had time to reflect after he left the army. I like to point to Mark Twain on the one hand, and Smedley Butler on the other, to demonstrate that there is a very powerful strain of dissent in the United States that we have to build on. But very few people know this. Today vast sections of Latin America have begun to rebel. In order to drive home the lessons, they have to come up with alternatives, and if even modest alternatives begin to work in Latin America, as they appear to be doing in Venezuela, it will be a serious setback for the economic policies of the empire.

The second big fissure is in the Arab east. It is important because of oil. In this region we now have a dual occupation—Palestine occupied by Israel and Iraq by the United States and Britain. This is not an easy problem to solve.

The third fissure is Afghanistan: They are tied down there; they will probably be forced to withdraw under the cover of a puppet regime; and the minute they go, chaos will reign.

As these fissures continue to open, we must hope a crucial element emerges: the challenge at home. The challenge in the heart of the United States takes place on different levels—culturally, politically, socially—but ultimately it has to find its way into official politics. You cannot just challenge from below. The movement from below has to find some reflection at the top—someone who can give voice to the aspirations of those at the bottom; that has not happened since George McGovern unsuccessfully ran for president.

Edward Said was fond of quoting a Gramsci dictum: "Pessimism of the intellect, optimism of the will." Does that inspire you?

Gramsci borrowed that from Romain Rolland—but yes, it does inspire me. We have to be hardheaded and realistic. There were a lot of fantasy politics in the past. The 1960s were great times, and I don't regret anything we did then, but there was a craziness as well. The Weather Underground and the Black Panthers believed you could challenge the empire with force and win—it was crazy. You cannot win unless you win over a majority, or at least a sizeable segment, of the population. We have got to win over that consent to our side; that's the key. Otherwise, we lose. Even when it works against us, we have to tell the truth, and we cannot raise false hopes. Capitalism is not cracking up today, and it may take a long while to do so. It won't disappear until people see an alternative with which to replace it. The one alternative they saw from 1917 to 1989 was the false dawn of communism.

The system we have now doesn't satisfy the needs of the majority in the United States or anywhere else in the world, but sooner or later alternatives will arise. We have to be patient.

5

Pakistan: The General Rules

In an article in New Left Review *entitled "The Colour Khaki," you talk about your native land, which you have called "janissary Pakistan," and the politics of a country that was created out of British India during the partition of 1947. What are some of the salient points of your piece?*

"Janissary" is a word only known by aficionados of the Ottoman Empire. This was the army the Ottomans created. Not strictly a mercenary army, it was used by the Ottomans to capture territory—to take large parts of the world. The salient feature of the janissary army was that it was predominantly comprised of non-Turkish people. So when I talk about janissary Pakistan, I'm saying that Pakistan and its army are the janissaries of the world's only empire today—that this is an army used by the

This interview, conducted in November 2003, has not previously been broadcast or published.

American empire. Sometimes I say in jest to Pakistani friends—many of the people I went to school with later became senior officers in the military—"When the United States needs a secular dictator, we provide one. When they need an Islamist dictator, we provide one. And I'm sure if one day they ask for a hermaphrodite dictator, we will provide one as well. The generals will find one and say, 'Here, sir. Here you are. Here's a hermaphrodite. He can run the country for you now.' "

I called the essay "The Colour Khaki": this brownish-green color, the color of the military uniform, now dominates Pakistan in every single way. The army, of course, is one of the legacies of the British Empire; the British didn't leave much behind, but they did leave us an army, a civil service, and a railway network, all of which still function to some degree. In Pakistan, which was formed in 1947, the national movement was very weak. The Punjab, the largest part of Pakistan, had been run by a combination of landlords during the empire, and while they continued to run it after the British left, their rule and their control were weak; therefore, the army played a very big role. So Pakistan, from its birth, was ruled by a military-bureaucratic complex. The civil servants basically dominated political life, with the army poised to take over if politics ever got out of control.

Pakistan's first military coup took place in 1958, to preempt an April 1959 election that the United States feared would put into power nationalist parties ready to

break Pakistan's security pacts with the United States—
which they *would* have done, incidentally. So they organized a military coup. It has been the same ever since, a
recurring cycle: a military dictatorship, a civilian government that promises a great deal and delivers very little,
and then another military dictatorship and another civilian government. The bulk of that country's life has been
dominated by military dictatorships—while elected rep-
resentatives have run the country for fifteen years, and
unaccountable bureaucrats and their tame front men for
eleven, the army has ruled for twenty-nine. Our current
dictator, General Pervez Musharraf, wears a suit and a tie
when he travels abroad, but the only base he has in the
country is his position as commander in chief of the Pakistani army. That's why the U.S. does business with him;
they've always preferred to deal with the army in Pakistan, because they know it well. Many of the officers were
trained at Fort Bragg and other American institutions,
and the Americans feel they can do business with them,
whereas with the politicians it's always a bit difficult.

*There is a historical analogy with Latin America and coun-
tries in the Middle East as well: this American alliance with the
military.*

The dictatorships in Latin America, in particular
those imposed during the Cold War, kept those countries
on the side of the United States. In Pakistan it's the army

that has done that. There were some doubts at the end of the Cold War, because the United States lost interest in Pakistan and Afghanistan; after the Russians had been defeated, the Americans didn't much care about the region—until September 11, of course. They had even been talking to the Taliban, but they weren't interested in Pakistan or its problems, and a section of the army— Islamists and fundamentalists who had worked closely with the United States against the Russians in Afghanistan—deeply resented this neglect.

We must never, ever forget the image of Zbigniew Brzezinski, Carter's national security advisor, standing on the border between Pakistan and Afghanistan, addressing a huge gathering of people with beards, telling them: Go and fight against the Russian infidel. Go and wage the jihad. God is on your side. People in Pakistan remember that, and they said, We worked together with the Americans and we liberated Afghanistan, and then they dumped us. This brutal, unceremonious dumping created a lot of anger, because people were genuinely under the illusion that the Americans were on their side—not realizing that empires always act in their own interest; they have no other motivation. That created a lot of anger.

It was during that phase of the Afghan conflict with the Russians that the Islamist groups in Pakistan armed themselves; they had never been armed before. A lot of money and weapons flowed through the country, and the Islamists became a menace to civil institutions, civilian life—killings took place. Then Sunni fundamentalist groups arose, which started bombing Shia mosques and killing Shias because they regarded them as heretics. Then the Shias began to organize. The country was awash with factional violence for many years. That was a legacy of General [Muhammad] Zia's rule, which completely disrupted the nation's political culture and political life. We are still paying a price for it.

Let me just add something that Brzezinski said later in the 1990s. When it became apparent that elements of the mujahedeen, which had been so warmly embraced, supported, and trained by the United States and its Pakistani mercenaries, had morphed into the Taliban, he asked rhetorically, Well, compared to the collapse of the Soviet Union, what's "a few stirred-up Muslims?"

It illustrated how out of touch he was with the stirred-up Muslims. The stirred-up Muslims finally came and hit New York and the Pentagon. This is what Chalmers Johnson described presciently as "blowback." No one has ever challenged Brzezinski on that particular remark; we will never see an editorial in the *New York Times* denouncing him for it. This is a recurring feature in U.S. foreign policy: their interests require an alliance with X or Y or Z; they go ahead without a thought about the consequences, for themselves or for the rest of the world.

Let's go back to the origins of Pakistan. It's one of the largest Muslim countries in the world—its population is around 150 million. Two key figures are Muhammad Iqbal and Muhammad Ali Jinnah. Start with Iqbal. He was born in 1873 and died in 1938. Why was he important and what role did he play in the formation of Muslim consciousness in South Asia?

I think one has to go back further to the Mughal Empire, which lasted from the sixteenth until the eighteenth century. Hundreds of years of Mughal imperial rule created a ruling elite. It was mixed, by and large, but certainly the Muslims were the ruling class. They were Muslim kings, and they ruled together with a Hindu, and later a Sikh, elite; even Aurangzeb, the most confessional-minded of the Mughal rulers, had all Hindus as his leading generals. It was not a confessionalism that was imposed, in any case, but large numbers of Hindus in India did convert to Islam, in reaction against the caste system. On paper, once you're a Muslim, you are equal before God—there are no distinctions of class or color inside Islam. Many people converted, and Islam—though always in the minority—became a major force in India.

The entry of the British and the collapse of the Mughal Empire ruined the livelihoods of large numbers of people—scribes, calligraphers, artisans—who worked around the court, eviscerating the Muslim elite. Slowly the perception took hold that Muslims were dispossessed, that they had nothing left. The British didn't treat them well either, and that provoked a mutiny, the first rebellion against the British, in 1857, which came close to success, incidentally. In some parts of India the British were defeated, but it was British technology—and the fact that they could win over elements of the native ruling classes—that finally won the day. This left a deep mark on the Muslims of India.

Gradually, currents within the Muslim community began to embrace modernity, to look toward the West in an attempt to learn something there. Syed Ahmed Khan was one of them. Muhammad Iqbal, whom you asked me about, was one of the great poets of the Indian subcontinent. Initially, Iqbal believed in a composite nationalism, which incorporated everyone—Hindu, Sikh, Muslim, Buddhist—to fight for a free India. In fact, he wrote the anthem of India, "Tarana-e-Hindi": "More beautiful than the rest of the world is our great nation of India." It is still sung today in parts of India, because it became the anthem of the nationalist movement. Iqbal and others became very disturbed when Mahatma Gandhi, great man though he was, began to use a great deal of Hindu imagery to awaken the Hindu masses. A group of Muslim politicians, including Iqbal and Muhammad Ali Jinnah, the founder of Pakistan, reacted quite strongly; they said, We never had any of this before. Why is Gandhi referring to Ram Raj and this and that? Suddenly they realized that the empire had created a competition between the two communities.

The Muslim League was set up in 1906 by British initiative. If you look at the founding document of the Muslim League, it says, We, the rulers and Muslim notables of India and *talukdars,* large landowners, have created this organization to foster a sense of loyalty to the British Empire. That's the founding document of the Muslim League—it was created to challenge nationalism. The Congress leaders, Gandhi and Nehru, not to mention Patel, made a lot of mistakes, in my opinion, by antagonizing sections of Muslims who could have been held together—but that would have meant concessions, serious concessions. That didn't happen. Iqbal formulated the idea of a Muslim nation in India; his theory was that we were two nations, but at the same time, he remained very aware of the internal class divisions. To his enormous credit, Iqbal—a poet—never forgot that in spite of the rift between Muslims and Hindus, the real division in India was between peasants and landlords. He was shocked by the treatment the peasants received, and he wrote this wonderful poem—I think the title was "Lenin's Interview with God." Lenin dies and goes up to heaven in the poem, and God says, Hi, Lenin. Nice to see you here. Why were you creating so much trouble on earth? Lenin gives God an explanation and says, God, don't you know what exists in the real world, the suffering? And God then gives this instruction to the Archangel Gabriel, which is one of the classic verses of Indian poetry. The original is in Urdu, and it goes something like this:

> *Arise, awake even the wretched of the earth*
> *Shake the foundations, tremble the walls*
> *of the mansions in which the wealthy sleep;*
> *And in every field where a peasant starves,*
> *There go and burn every bushel of wheat.*

This particular verse became a favorite of the progressive movement—I remember hearing from old peasant leaders that when this verse was recited to the peasants, there would be tears in their eyes. This was the poet who said at the same time that a separate Muslim homeland was necessary. Initially, there was no big fervor for it amongst the Muslim masses. In the parts of the country where there were large Muslim populations—the North-West Frontier Province, Baluchistan, and the Punjab, which was of course equally divided—there was no big enthusiasm for Pakistan. The fervor came from those parts of India where Muslims were a small minority: Central India, Uttar Pradesh Province, places where Muslim landlords and intellectuals feared that after Indian independence they would be totally overwhelmed by Hindu domination. They did not realize that they might not have been overwhelmed had large Muslim states been part of an Indian federation.

What was decisive in the formation of Pakistan had very little to do with the real needs of Muslims, but a great deal to do with the Second World War. During the war, Gandhi lost his nerve: After the fall of Singapore he thought the British Empire was finished and the Japanese were going to march in. It was a very cynical operation on his part; he figured that, with the Japanese coming, he should start a movement in order to attain some position of strength from which to negotiate with the Japanese. So Gandhi launched the Quit India movement in August 1942. The British were shocked, because prior to that the Indians had been negotiating with their conquerors. Nehru's position was very interesting. He said that India would defend the Allies in the Second World War because fascism was the enemy—but that only a free India could make that decision; it could not be an imposed decision. If you get out now and give India its freedom, Nehru suggested, free India will decide to back you in the war. The British, however, weren't prepared to do that. They said, privately, You will get your independence the minute the war is over, but back us now. Gandhi, obstinate, said no.

The British sent a big delegation to see Gandhi, just before the launching of the Quit India movement. Sir Stafford Cripps and leading British progressives went in 1942 and promised him anything after the war. He refused to make a deal. When Cripps said he was being given a blank check by the British, Gandhi replied, in his quaking voice, "What's the point of a blank check from a bank that is failing?" In other words, he misjudged the situation. He wasn't the only one. People thought the Japanese would come in and take India, and that made the British livid.

This is when the Muslim League was used to support the war. The Muslim League began to mobilize people, suggesting that if they fought the war, the British would owe them. I've always felt—and most historians don't even talk about it—that this deal struck by the Muslim League and the British during the Second World War, in a pretty decisive period for the British Empire, forced them to give the Muslims something, so they gave them this moth-eaten, truncated state. It's worth remembering that up until 1946, a year before partition, Jinnah was prepared to accept some sort of confederated solution, provided—this was expressed secretly—he would be prime minister of united India. Jinnah was ailing. Gandhi cleverly at that point said, Let's make Jinnah the prime minister; agree to it. Nehru and Patel said, No. How can we have this? So, pettiness. And narrow-mindedness dominated. But in 1946—Pakistani historians don't like to acknowledge this, but it's true—Jinnah was prepared to make a deal, because he knew what the score was.

Consider the North-West Frontier Province. Eighty percent of the population voted for Ghaffar Khan, a Congress leader—this Muslim-dominated province was voting for the Congress right up until 1946, and the votes were only changed by intimidation by the Muslim

League, who bullied, imprisoned, and killed people. There was a famous massacre in a bazaar in Peshawar to force people into the other direction. There was no mass support for Pakistan; it is a state created from the top. That is why the Pakistani elite, from 1947 onwards, suffered from what we can just call a big inferiority complex about India, worrying that everything was dominated by India; they couldn't see it otherwise. Just like Israel, formed in 1948; another confessional state planted from the top, obsessed with the Arab world, that can't think about anything else. And General Zia ul-Haq, the most brutal military dictator we've had, used to compare Pakistan and Israel all the time; he would say, Like Israel, we are a tough state. Yes, we are confessional states; yes, we will build tough armies, and so on.

From the very beginning, Pakistan decided that anything India supported, they couldn't go along with. They had to prove themselves by constantly differentiating themselves from India. When India was nonaligned—when Jawaharlal Nehru initiated the nonaligned movement—Pakistan signed a security pact with the United States; the first one was in 1951, and another in 1953. Pakistan's prime minister, Mohammad Ali Bogra, led a demonstration in Karachi welcoming the arrival of U.S. wheat, with signs saying "Thank You, America"—that's when the whole thing started. Gradually the hold of the British Empire in Pakistan came to an end, and the United States took over, just as it did in Saudi Arabia and many other parts of the world, and Pakistan essentially became an American satellite.

Back to Jinnah, who was an English-trained barrister who could not speak any Indian language, not even Urdu, the national language of Pakistan. He became that country's first president in 1947. He died a year later. But let's just go back a bit further and reconnect with something you said about Gandhi's tactics of reviving Hindu terminology and things like fasting and vegetarianism and bhajans, *which are Hindu devotional songs. Jinnah, apparently, who was a member of the Congress Party, warned him in an often quoted comment, "Mr. Gandhi, don't go in that direction. Don't go toward religion. Keep Congress secular."*

Jinnah was basically a totally secular guy; in fact, he was an agnostic. But once he became leader of the Muslim League, it was impossible for him to say this in public. People don't like hearing this today in Pakistan, but whenever Jinnah, who lived in Bombay, used to travel to Lahore—he was a well-known and distinguished lawyer—he always used to stay at Faletti's Hotel, an old colonial hotel with lovely large rooms all built on one level. People used to ask him, Why don't you stay with friends? There are hundreds of homes that would welcome you, Mr. Jinnah. And he would say, I have to stay in Faletti's because they do the best bacon and eggs.

Explain the significance of pork in Islam.

Pork is totally forbidden in Islam. It's *haram*. The great leader of this Muslim nation was not only an agnostic but defied every taboo. And, of course, as you said, he couldn't speak any of the languages. English was his only language. He couldn't speak Punjabi, Sindhi, or Urdu. His Urdu was painful. My Urdu is bad—my Punjabi is good but my Urdu is not—but when I listened to Jinnah's tapes, I felt like a master of the Urdu language; he spoke it in a very stuttering way. This is the man who was the founder of the Islamic state. Just like the Zionists, incidentally, like David Ben-Gurion and Moshe Dayan, who were not at all religious. All these people were of implacable temperament, very hard-bitten guys, not religious, totally secular. So a Jewish state, Israel, and a Muslim state, Pakistan, both created by secular politicians because it suited their needs to do so.

Jinnah would have been quite happy to remain a member of the Congress Party if it had not begun to use Hindu imagery. But it was more than that: Gandhi used Hindu rhetoric to mobilize the Indian masses, because he felt it was the only way to do so—he was wrong, I think, but that's how he started the civil disobedience movement. This is the other thing that upset Jinnah, who was an elitist. He said, Democracy is something we will give to the people. He viewed the participation of people from below in this movement with distaste. He would wear this monocle and look down on even his equals. He found it distasteful—and unnecessary—to involve the masses, and felt that independence would only be obtained by negotiating with the British as equals. He did not like either of these developments, so he resigned from the Congress. Jinnah, who Gandhi said was the ambassador of Hindu-Muslim unity, was the man who finally formed Pakistan.

And Iqbal, the great poet, was born in Sialkot, in your home province of Punjab. But he is closely identified with Lahore, and that's where he's buried, right next to the Badshahi Masjid. He died in 1938, but before his death, he came up with the term "Pakistan"—the Punjab, Afghan, Kashmir, Sindh.

I think the actual word "Pakistan," inspired by Iqbal, was coined by a Muslim student in London, Rehmat Ali, who added up the words and came up with Pakistan. They thought it worked nicely, because it symbolized the provinces, plus the word *pak* means pure—Pakistan was the land of the pure. That's how it happened. When Iqbal died in 1938, he was mourned by many; he had a massive funeral. To this day, no one ever mentions that he died of syphilis because he used to visit the whorehouses of Lahore a bit too often, something not very well known. He, too, was not a great believer, in other words, in purity. So this great poet, who died of a venereal disease, left behind a country called the land of the pure. There are many ironies in our world.

Pakistan is like Israel—both were controlled by the British and both were created out of partitions which have left an enormous legacy of death, destruction, dislocation, and refugees.

The Israeli example is, of course, very well known because of great Palestinian voices like Mahmoud Darwish, Edward Said, and others. Here I would just like to say about Edward, whom I loved dearly—his greatest accomplishment was not his literary theory; it was the fact that Palestine became his cause, and he became the chronicler of a dispossessed nation, a people without a homeland. That's what won him the respect all over the world; he was the only real historian Palestine possessed who was not marked by the corruption and intrigues of Arafat or the other Palestinian leaders. He kept the cause of Palestine alive and explained what had happened.

As far as the Indian partition is concerned, nearly two million people died—there is a big debate, is it one or two million?—I say, "Look, I don't know. It's just as bad." I use the figure of nearly two million, because we know that the deaths of lots of poor people went unrecorded; they were buried in mass graves. Not a single monument marks the victims of partition: the Muslims, the Hindus and Sikhs who were killed in Bengal and the Punjab. Neither India nor Pakistan honored the victims.

One of the most moving poems written about partition was by an eighteen-year-old Sikh girl who had to leave Lahore because it was now being partitioned. She saw the killings and burnings. And she wrote this great poem that evokes the memory of the great Sufi poet Waris Shah, who wrote the epic Heer and Ranjha, which is still sung all over the Punjab in India and in Pakistan. Shah, a seventeenth-century mystic poet, wrote about the love of a woman for a man and described the scream of the woman, Heer, forced into a marriage against her will—the first line of Waris Shah's poem is, "As he mounted the wedding palanquin, she screamed." That scream dominates Punjabi culture. This eighteen-year-old girl refers to that poem, and she says, "Waris Shah, when one woman screamed, you wrote hundreds of verses to commemorate her. Today, thousands and thousands of women are dying, corpses are floating down our rivers. Can't we open a new book from your page to commemorate this and open the eyes of the people? Blood flows down the Chenab—one of the great rivers of the Punjab." Other poets also described the partition, as in Faiz Ahmed Faiz's famous opening lines after partition in 1947: "This mottled dawn, this ugly dawn / This is not what we set out for when we started for independence." The poets have commemorated it, but the historical memory of the tragedy has not been preserved.

Without the British Empire there would have been no Israel and there would have been no partition of India. Who knows what else would be different? These two states, which have brought so much misery and suffering, would not exist. But these states are now both nuclear states, and nothing can dismantle them.

I'm Armenian. My mother went through the genocide of 1915. My father fled in 1912. They met in 1921 and settled in New York. But there was always this memory of the old country. We call it yergeer *in Armenian. It was almost a magical place. And then years later, when I went to India and lived there and traveled to Pakistan as well, I met many people who reminded me not just of my parents but of all my relatives who had survived the genocide, who were always longing for* yergeer. *I would meet Punjabis from West Punjab now living in East Punjab, and waxing, perhaps romantically, about how wonderful it was and how the water was so clean and the air was so crisp. It really resonated with me and connected with my own background.*

I was about four years old when partition took place, so I don't have any real memories of it. My family was from a region that became Pakistan, so we did not have to move. But as I was growing up, I remember traveling around Lahore, sitting in the back of the car with my parents in the front driving. And I would often hear my father say to my mother, pointing to a house, "Brijinder"—a Sikh name—"lived there," or, "Do you remember who

used to live in that house?" Through my parents, I realized the scale of what had happened, that these were
houses in which Hindus and Sikhs had lived—that we had
been deprived of a multicultural society. Pakistan had become monocultural. Even though Lahore was still a great
city, my generation could never appreciate what it had
been. People talked about Lahore as the Paris of the East,
a big, cosmopolitan center, and we had no sense of this
save what we gleaned from our parents. Most people
didn't even talk about it.

There is a very moving story of a professor of literature at Government College, Lahore, who had taken his
whole family to Simla, in the Himalayan foothills, for the
summer holidays, when partition happened. He couldn't
even come back. People said: "You will be killed. Don't
come back." Many years later, his daughter is sent to Lahore. Her father is ill and dying. All he wants is to get back
his books—he wonders what has happened to his library.
So she comes to see my parents, who knew the professor,
and my father says, "Let's go." They go to the family
house, which she can still remember from her childhood,
and it is now occupied by a right-wing lawyer. I'll name
him: Ejaz Batalvi. He was one of the lawyers who prose-
cuted Bhutto during the Zia period and encouraged the
use of fake evidence that led to Bhutto's hanging. This
lawyer owns the house of this old Hindu Government
College professor in Model Town, Lahore.

She goes into the house—Batalvi can't quite say no

to her—and all her father's books are still up on the shelves. So she takes them down, and where it reads "Ex Libris" and her father's name—all those pieces have been cut out. She says to him, "All my father wants are these books. Could I take some of them back?" And he says, "No." My father takes her on one side and says, "Let's leave. It's not worth it." There are people like that, who just took over new identities by stealing and looting the property that had been left behind.

We were cut off from each other. You couldn't go to India from Pakistan; it was just a tragedy. The borders were always sealed. When I was at Oxford, I made Indian friends; it was the first time I had met Hindus and Sikhs. And then, when I went to India for the first time in the early 1970s, people found out I was in town. I was invited to dinner every single night by Sikh families. The kids would tell me, "Our parents want to see you because they knew your parents." Sumptuous meals would be prepared, and they would sit me down after dinner with a glass of whiskey in my hand and say, "Just talk about Lahore." That was really moving.

You mentioned Zulfikar Ali Bhutto. He was prime minister during the 1970s, and was overthrown in a military coup by Zia ul-Haq. That's had a searing legacy on Pakistan's development. Eqbal Ahmad, the great Pakistani scholar/activist, often talked about Zia, and the cruelty of his regime.

The particular culture of Pakistan was wrecked by Zia. Under his regime the Afghan war was waged, and he was encouraged by the United States to promote Islam. During his time in power, things happened in Pakistan that had not happened before: Political activists from the opposition parties were publicly flogged, there were public hangings—can you imagine?—in the late 1970s. He did all this quite deliberately, to brutalize the country's culture and intimidate the opposition. After two years, he hanged Bhutto, on a fake murder charge. Bhutto had many weaknesses, but he was the country's first elected prime minister. They hanged him because they were scared that if they left him alive he could not be crushed—that he might rise again and have his revenge. When Zia took over, and he began to assemble these false charges and rigged cases against Bhutto, people used to say, This is going to end badly. And you would say, Why? There are two men, and only one coffin: one of them has to go. The guy who provided false testimony against Bhutto at his trial was his own head of intelligence, Masood Sheikh, a total rogue, whom Bhutto should never have trusted in the first place. He testified that Bhutto had ordered a murder.

Bhutto was hanged by Zia, but Masood was too scared to live in Pakistan. His CIA friends gave him refuge in California. While I was in Los Angeles a couple weeks ago, a couple came up to me, totally out of the blue, and said, "Did you know him?" I said, "I don't know him. I don't want to know him," and I told them his story. They said, "Oh, how funny. He used to come and talk to our children and tell them stories." I said, "Did he ever tell them the story of what he did in Pakistan and why he had to leave?"

The reign of General Zia—the takeover, the executions, the judicial assassination of Bhutto, the brutalization of the country's culture—created the Islamist organizations that began to dominate the country during this time. The Afghan war brought a massive amount of arms into Pakistan—the United States was so determined to defeat the Russians that money was no object—and these guns were trafficked all over the world, sold everywhere. When the Defense Department finally sent in auditors from the States to check on the situation, the Pakistani military arranged to blow up the big arms dump at Ojhri, near Islamabad. People told me later, "We thought India had declared war. There were rockets going off all over the place." The military claimed it had been an accidental fire, so when the American auditors arrived there was nothing to investigate—the Pakistanis said, "There was a terrible accidental explosion a few nights before you arrived."

Bhutto's daughter, Benazir, later became prime minister of Pakistan. She was forced out of office over huge corruption charges, and she was tried in absentia. She's now living in Eu-

rope. Then there was a civilian government in the 1990s led by Nawaz Sharif, until he was overthrown in a coup by General Pervez Musharraf. What happened?

Benazir's government and that of Nawaz Sharif came into power in Pakistan in a new world—a neoliberal world. This is a world where only money matters, a world where politicians all over the world are seen as corrupt and linked intimately to corporations. In Pakistan, which was already a corrupt society anyway, politicians took this as a green light. People used to say to Benazir, Lots of people are saying you and your husband are very corrupt, and she said, Well, politicians are corrupt everywhere— why shouldn't we make some money? Publicly she denied it, but privately they looted the country. They stole billions from this poor country, which could have been used for health and education.

That's why many people hate them, because they know what happened. The Pakistan People's Party came to power in the name of the poor; the poor voted for them. In the election that Benazir lost, participation dropped by 75 percent. The poor would no longer come out to vote for her. They would not vote for her opponents, but they refused to vote for her. Turnout in that election was around 25 percent; people just vowed they would not vote for these politicians. Nawaz Sharif, her opponent, was equally corrupt. He was overthrown by Musharraf, for bad reasons, I think: not because he was corrupt but because, to his credit, being a businessman, he saw the logic of making a deal with India to open up trade relations and relax the tensions. But he did it without the army's approval, and they deposed him and put Musharraf in power. Clinton was initially a bit hostile to him. But after September 11, the general became yet another valued ally in the war against terror.

What was the payoff to Musharraf and the country for his support of the United States?

All restrictions were lifted: weaponry began to flow again, aid began to flow again, a lot of money arrived from America to get the regime on the right track. Musharraf could then say, "Look, I brought Pakistan into the world again. We were a pariah state for some time, but now, by backing the United States, this is what's happened."

It was because of the testing of nuclear weapons in May 1998 that the U.S. imposed sanctions on Pakistan.

The embargo was imposed on Pakistan because it developed and tested nuclear weapons. But that has all been forgotten; the valued ally in the war against terror can possess as many weapons of mass destruction as he likes—it's not a problem. Meanwhile, inside the country nothing much is happening. Musharraf is a secular guy; he's not an Islamist, which is a sort of boon, I guess. But unless and until the political leaders of Pakistan do something to improve the conditions of the people, nothing is going to change. It's the same cycle. People are becoming more and more demoralized and embittered, with both the politicians and the army.

He did have some advice, actually, for the United States. He's been rather timid in his comments, but he did talk about the need for the United States to change its approach in the war on terrorism. He said that the root causes of terror and extremism need to be addressed—that unjust situations in which Muslim peoples are victims of state terror are being ignored.

I wonder where he picked that up? Perhaps from one of my articles in the Pakistani press. I'm glad he said that, in any case. But it is just a small remark. I think he feels obliged to say these things from time to time because there is a big Islamist opposition in Pakistan, which now controls two provinces. For the first time, the Islamists have acquired a real electoral legitimacy in Pakistan, because Musharraf has been incapable of resisting American pressure. The Islamists have come to power in these provinces because they are the only political force in the country that opposed the occupation of Afghanistan and mobilized people against the war in Iraq. No one else is doing it.

And the United States now has troops and bases inside the country.

The Americans have troops and bases all over Pakistan, and everyone knows that. That's why, when there was the threat of another war between India and Pakistan, I said, It will never happen, because the Indians know that to attack Pakistan, when all its military and air force bases are occupied by the United States, would be insane. It's just not going to happen. The Indians are just putting pressure on the United States, to remind them, "We're here, too. Don't totally ignore us." But the American military presence in Pakistan has created a great deal of anger there, and if the occupation authorities in Afghanistan do make a deal with a section of the Taliban and dump the Northern Alliance, God knows what the result of that is going to be. One immediate outcome could be a narco-war between armed groups of drug barons.

Since the partition of the subcontinent in 1947 into two states, there has been a consistent problem plaguing both countries: Kashmir. Two-thirds of Kashmir is controlled by India, one-third by Pakistan. There have been a couple of wars fought over it. In 1989, a rebellion started in the province; tens of thousands of Kashmiris have been killed since then. There are hundreds of thousands of Indian security forces there. It has been a flash

*point and a trigger for war, and for potential wars of even greater
magnitude. Can you encapsulate the core of the problem that exists around Kashmir and suggest a possible solution?*

Kashmir is a large Muslim-majority state. It was not
allowed to decide if it wanted to be part of India or Pakistan: It was taken militarily by India, but Jawaharlal
Nehru promised its great nationalist leader, Sheikh Abdullah, that the Kashmiris would be allowed the right to
national self-determination. The UN passed a resolution
suggesting a plebiscite, but India subsequently prevented
that from ever taking place. Nehru was coming close to
it, but he died at the worst possible moment, and his successors have not even considered it. So the Kashmiris do
feel oppressed; seventy thousand Kashmiris have died
since 1989, and the situation is a complete mess.

When I talk to secular Kashmiri leaders, they insist
that they do not want all the trappings of independence,
like an independent army and an independent foreign
policy; they want to live free of outside interference in a
unified Kashmir. The only way this will happen is if the
five big states of South Asia agree to a South Asian union
using and improving the model of the European Union,
within which framework you can solve the Kashmir
problem—and also the Tamil problem in Sri Lanka—by
guaranteeing these regions autonomy. For this, however,
you need real visionaries as leaders. It's certainly some-

thing that the movements for global justice and intellectuals should be arguing for, a South Asian union to take
advantage of the strengths of this region and to bring people together instead of dividing them and sending them
to fight each other. I think here we have a possibility of a
solution, but what we lack are leaders.

*The five states would be Bangladesh, Sri Lanka, Nepal,
India, and Pakistan.*

Those are the five states, of which India is the largest.
But they would form a core in Asia that would be very
strong and powerful. The great empire prefers to balkanize countries so it can better rule them, and it's important that regions begin to think of how to strengthen
themselves. The Far Eastern sector, I would argue, will
ultimately need to do that as well. This is the only way you
can solve your own problems, aid your populations, and
resist the depredations of the empire. We must begin to
re-imagine Asia.

*Pakistan seems to be a fragile state that's on pins and nee-
dles; it's wracked with internal divisions. You've talked about the
Shia-Sunni sectarian violence, the huge surge of Islamic fundamentalism in the country, the weapons and drugs, the legacy of
the Afghan mujahedeen. Twenty years ago, you wrote a book won-
dering about the future of Pakistan. What's your perspective
today?*

My book was titled *Can Pakistan Survive?* But that was a time when we didn't know what was going to happen in Iran and Afghanistan, or in India, where Hindu fundamentalists have been in power. Pakistan, like Israel, is now a nuclear power, and it's impossible for anything to happen to these states—they will survive. One therefore has to devise means whereby the military power can be neutralized and coexistence can take place. In Israel, this means a free and independent Palestine and an Israeli withdrawal to the 1967 frontiers. In the case of Pakistan, it means a serious initiative by Indian and Pakistani leaders towards a South Asian union, to reduce the military budget and begin to help the people.

6

Enablers of Empire

*W*e *are sitting in one of the cradles of learning in the United States, Harvard University. Its endowment probably exceeds the budget of many countries of the world. Sometimes people talk about the military-industrial complex, Eisenhower's famous term, but they never mention the academy. What role does it play in empire?*

The academy plays a very important role; historically, it has been one of the foremost pillars of empire. A critical academy also exists, but by and large the academy reflects and represents the so-called virtues of manifest destiny and empire. Harvard is a particularly interesting case: The university was built on land that once belonged to Native Americans, though its founders were prone to saying that "we came to virgin lands." It was reminiscent of strains we find familiar from Zionist thought; refugees

This interview, conducted in February 2004, was broadcast on *Alternative Radio*.

coming to a "land without people" and seizing it, trying to forget and ignore the horrors inflicted on Native Americans. Harvard as an institution has been part and parcel of the establishment for a long time, throughout the Cold War. Obviously, there are always critical voices. One has to say that: there are good critical voices, but the overwhelming bulk of the academy, let's say, is like plasticine—it goes with the empire, it molds itself accordingly.

I'm thinking of people like Samuel Huntington, Francis Fukuyama, and this aging totem Bernard Lewis. We are now told that there is a Lewis doctrine—the *Wall Street Journal* tells us that the Lewis doctrine is bringing democracy to the Muslim East. This is a man who gave talks during the Cold War, in the 1950s, in which he insisted that Islam and communism were twins. At a time when the American empire was actually using Islam to try and defeat communism, Lewis was so hostile to Islam that he attempted for the first and only time to go against the establishment consensus—he was worried about its close relations with Islam. Islam and communism, he said then, are twins: they're very similar; they have similar collectivist approaches. These are the people that have basically dominated the academy, and even more objective scholars have found it difficult to buck the trend.

This is in addition to the developments in the academy since the collapse of the Communist world: the popularity of postmodernism and of cultural studies, both of which denigrate the study and pursuit of history as a grand narrative. The resurgence of the American empire, and the fact that Bush and his neocons are not scared to nakedly parade their strength, to say, "We do these things because we can, because it suits our interests, and that's what matters"—this is a problem for that wing of the academy that thought it could live in its own world. It wanted to be critical, but it also desired not to get involved in big debates: politics and history, these were old things. They were on to new things. They would discuss tiny little fragments, tiny little episodes. They would discuss gender, they would discuss identity, and these things were far more important. History has shown that this is now not the case, and the academy has to become more critical if it's going to move forward.

Let me add a new type of figure that the empire needs and the academy nourishes. A new species has emerged from the crisis in the Arab East. I like to call him the "house Arab": men like Fouad Ajami and Kanan Makiya, who want to please the empire and serve its needs, and, in the case of Ajami, are completely and totally shameless in the way they abase themselves before the empire. These men say things that many Americans think but wouldn't dare to say in public; this is their value, that they are willing to voice sentiments that even ruling-class, establishment Americans would prefer not to articulate, however much they may agree privately. These people find their niche in our debased media, which needs people like this, to demonstrate that there are Arabs who are on our side—look how intelligent they are. They are intelligent because they say what people want to hear; their intelligence is determined exclusively by their instrumentality. They are useful, and therefore they have to be used.

Many people fall into this trap, even good people. My dear friend in Pakistan, Ahmed Rashid, fell into it temporarily after the occupation of Afghanistan, because his book on the Taliban reached new heights—it was needed. The Americans needed to study a book on the Taliban, and Ahmed's book was it. I'm very fond of Ahmed, and he's not like Fouad Ajami and Kanan Makiya. But even people like him are tempted by empire, because they have lost faith in the capacity of ordinary people to emancipate themselves without the aid of American intervention. I haven't spoken to Ahmed for some time, and I hope he has pulled back. The house Arabs are the embedded intellectuals of the empire. That's where they see their future, and they probably dream of rising further. They are very happy people; there are no problems for them at all.

Ajami is of Lebanese origin. He's a professor at Johns Hopkins University and a frequent guest on network talk shows. He is, in fact, a commentator on CBS News, *advising Dan Rather on the intricacies of Arabs, Islam, and Muslims. I'm interested that you use the term "house Arab," because that evokes the mem-*

ory of Malcolm X. He made a distinction between field Negroes and house Negroes. The field Negroes were rebellious and clamoring for the manor to burn down, whereas the house Negroes were loyal servants; if the manor were on fire, they would seek to put it out.

Of course, "house Arab" is derived entirely from Malcolm's great description of old collaborators with the empire. I would say that the house Arabs are worse than what Malcolm called house Negroes, because house Negroes, after all, were slaves. They were the slaves idealized in *Gone with the Wind* and other books—totally loyal. But one has to remember that they were slaves, whereas the house Arabs are free. Their actions are entirely voluntary, and that makes what they do much worse; they have lost all sense of objectivity. I wouldn't expect them to support the Iraqi resistance, but, for God's sake, they should at least stand back and see what's going on, see that what's happening in the Middle East is a total and complete disaster. But these people don't operate like that. They want to be advisers to the empire, to say, "You're not doing it well enough. This is how you could improve it. People will be killed, yes. So what?" This is the role some of these people play.

There is a new breed of person who believes this is the only way to integrate into North American society, whether through the academy or by producing books that are championed by the media. Irshad Manji, a Canadian

Muslim, has written a book called *The Trouble with Islam*. She spoke at Harvard yesterday at the same time as I did, and I heard that her talk was packed with Zionists, who spent the whole evening denouncing Palestinian terrorism: this is the use that is made of these people. I'm very critical of all religions, including Islam, but to allow yourself to be used in this fashion and to wallow in it, there is something a bit disgusting about that.

Historically empires have always needed native informants to provide information.

This is a sort of historical truth, which has applied to every single empire. Foreign occupiers trying to take over a land cannot do it on their own; even the Romans needed local support, and they got it. They rewarded people with Roman citizenship, regardless of race or color; you could be Nubian and receive citizenship if you worked for the Romans.

Look at the Spanish conquest of Mexico: Malinche, who helped Cortés, became his mistress, and told him the secrets of Tenochtitlán, the Aztec capital. If you look at Diego Rivera's phenomenal paintings in the Ministry of Education, the murals that recount the history of Mexico, you can see that he depicts her basically as a tart: She is standing there a bit bare, with her legs showing. This collaborationism has a long history.

As I discussed earlier, even the British Empire—the last big, serious empire—stationed no more than thirty-six thousand British soldiers in India; they could not have ruled hundreds of millions on the subcontinent without native support. The British were very clever imperialists. They marshaled support by changing the social structure of the country, creating a landlord class by passing a whole series of acts.

There was a layer of privileged village elders, who had held the right to collect taxes since the Moghul era—revenue collectors, we might call them; tax men. Seeing that this was a powerful group, the British gave them property rights to the territory in which they collected taxes, creating a class of landlords that—especially in Bengal, Punjab, Uttar Pradesh, and Kashmir—became a rock-solid pillar on which the British Empire could rely. When that coalition began to break up, the empire broke up as well. Without collaborators, empires cannot function.

If a sizeable segment of the Kurds or the Shia in Iraq today were to come out against the empire now and join the resistance, this occupation would end—within a matter of months, not years. The process has begun. Collaborators are extremely important for empires: without them, empires couldn't exist. That's the reality of it. To go back to Malcolm's point, if there had been constant slave rebellions, had no cohort of house niggers come into existence, the South would have been in continuous revolt, and the whole system would have collapsed, even before the Civil War.

Kanan Makiya has been described by the Guardian *as "Iraq's most eminent dissident thinker." He had an audience with the commander in chief, George Bush, in which he told the president that the Americans would be greeted with "sweets and flowers" when they entered Iraq.*

There's a story behind that *Guardian* profile: The journalist was instructed to interview Makiya as a sop to the foreign office—it was torturous, apparently. She said that some on the paper wanted an even more servile and sycophantic portrait of Makiya, but she had toned it down. The reason for this is very simple: when the states involved are gearing up for war, they need to promote people who will fulfill their needs. Makiya masqueraded around as this tortured, tormented soul who had only the interests of Iraq and nothing else at heart. I know him—we were in the same political organization in the 1970s. He always was slightly self-centered, I have to say, and this is still the case. This sort of messianism which he decries in others is very dominant in him. What made him was the book he wrote, *The Republic of Fear,* which became a key book during the first Gulf War. I'm glad to say that we rejected it at Verso—we were prescient even then. Makiya first submitted it to Verso, but we thought it an unbalanced book.

Robin Blackburn, one of the editors, wrote a ten-page comment, outlining the book's problems, and Makiya then took it away. We would have made a lot of money, but in retrospect, I'm glad we didn't take it on, because though I don't deny that there are some interesting things in the book—one can't rubbish the whole project—one of its central themes is that Iraq was better off under the British Empire. There are passages in that book praising Emir Feisal as an enlightened ruler. At that point, during the Gulf War, Makiya decided that the only future for Iraq was as an imperial satrapy, and for that, he has been duly rewarded. Looking at the mess that has been created, we can see the fingerprints of Makiya, Ajami, and other lesser-known house Arabs—only partially, as we shouldn't exaggerate the influence of these people—who encouraged this invasion with the promise that American troops would be welcomed with open arms. They couldn't deliver, because they don't know Iraq; they're out of touch with Iraq. They failed to realize that even the Shia in southern Iraq, who loathed Sad-dam, were not prepared to welcome the occupiers with flowers.

Makiya should know better. His mother is British, but his father hails from Iraq and is a very distinguished and well-known architect who built some buildings for Saddam Hussein before leaving the country. Now his son is insisting that Americans bomb these structures his own father built—a scenario that the good doctor in Vienna would have had a lot of fun trying to analyze.

The notion that empires act out of an enlightened interest in the state of the world has always been nonsense—this is what people like Kanan Makiya and other house Arabs totally ignore. An elementary fact of political life, throughout history, is that empires act in their own interests. This is the only thing they care about. Even when they have to take over a country and remold it, they do it because it suits their purposes—they don't intervene for the good of some country, but because they need to. Forgetting this is a big, big weakness with the house Arabs. They also forget that the British Empire, for the last forty or fifty years of its life, had to confront the growing tide of nationalism and communism, which was sparked off by the victory of the Russian Revolution. Just as the victory of the French Revolution in the eighteenth century inspired big slave uprisings in Haiti and elsewhere in the Caribbean and led to the first big slave victory under Toussaint L'Ouverture, the Russian Revolution sparked off a wave of nationalist uprisings all over the colonial world. This is what brought the empire to a quick end—one shouldn't forget that.

Makiya, who is a professor at Brandeis University in Boston, is—like Fouad Ajami and Bernard Lewis—a frequent guest on the talk shows.

Obviously, they get jobs in the U.S. universities. They dominate the airwaves because the empire needs them. It's important to put them on television, so Americans can say, "We are not the ones calling for war—it's Arab people themselves." That's the role these men play, and best of luck to them. Their fortunes will rise and fall with those of the people they serve. Iraq is now a disaster. How will it be explained? I'm sure that a narcissist like Makiya will say, "It's a disaster because they didn't do exactly as I advised them to do. If only they had followed my advice to the letter." Excuse me—they did follow your advice. They invaded Iraq. It's people like you who couldn't deliver anything. Ahmed Chalabi promised to deliver Iraq to the Israelis and said, Within six months of my being in power, we will recognize Israel. Well, boy, you've been there for more than six months, and even under a puppet regime you don't have the guts to recognize Israel. That's the reality.

Let me ask you about V.S. Naipaul, the Trinidad-born, Indian-origin writer, who has been living in Britain since the early 1950s. He's a Nobel Prize winner, celebrated for his many novels, but he's also written some nonfiction books, one particularly on Islam, called Among the Believers. *How do you see Naipaul in this galaxy of punditry?*

Sir Vidya Naipaul. He is a strange person—very different from these people, actually. He is of a different generation: He was born in the 1930s, grew up in

Trinidad in the 1930s and 1940s, moved to Britain in the 1950s, and adopted the colonial mode.

A kind of brown sahib, as they used to refer to it?

That's what he wanted to be. In fact, he wanted to be more English than the English. What he has in his favor, which we must never deny him—Edward Said and I used to talk about him a great deal—he is a very brilliant writer. We had to agree that he was a very brilliant writer. Edward would say, "He's much better than many of the novelists who came of age in the 1970s and 1980s—he just writes much better." This we must never take from him; I have enormous respect for him as a writer and a novelist. I don't agree with his politics, which are, of course, very reactionary, and he goes out of his way to taunt and provoke those he doesn't like. Vidya's hostility to the world of Islam has been slightly mitigated by the fact that, on his last trip to Pakistan, he met a much younger woman named Nadira, who was showing him around the country, and fell madly in love with her. The joke in Pakistan is that in order to marry her he had to convert to Islam. They say that Nadira would never have married him had he not converted. Whenever I go to Lahore and Karachi, people want to wager on this, and I say, "Show me the evidence, because this could be very entertaining." No evidence emerges, though dear Nadira is certainly a believer. She's not an atheist, she is a believer. She takes the Koran quite seriously. So if Sir Vidya Naipaul is a secret Muslim, we will find out one day.

The role he plays now is minimal. He is basically the grand old man of letters. During the early days of the government headed by the Bharatiya Janata Party—a right-wing Hindu fundamentalist party—Naipaul made some pretty appalling statements that were sympathetic to that government, claiming that Hindus had been persecuted by invading Muslim conquerors—a load of nonsense, quite honestly. That whole history has been turned upside down; if you listen to serious historians of India, like Romila Thapar, you see that invasions and migrations were the norm in that period all over the world. The invaders—whether the Indo-Europeans early on, or later the Muslims—came and mingled, and the societies changed; there was a cultural synthesis. There has been a constant attempt to rewrite history by the Hindutva people to bring it into accord with their modern needs, which Naipaul has sometimes supported. I think later he felt slightly ashamed of it, denied that he supported this government, and said he was horrified by the widespread killings and violence against Muslims in Gujarat in 2002. He is basically not a political person. He's essentially a cultural conservative.

"If they hate us, it's because they're backward"—this is a classic imperial theme.

In fact, this is always the theme taken up by imperial conquerors. We are conquering you, and by that fact we are superior, because were we not, how could we have conquered you? This has not, historically, always been the case. Genghis Khan created and built the world's largest empire: He took large parts of the world, his heirs took China and Iran, he marched into parts of India, he was at the gates of Europe, took Russia, took the Ukraine. His heirs took Baghdad in the thirteenth century, but the Mongols were a people without even a written language. They occupied countries, and one of the first things they did was to destroy the written word. They burned libraries, because they knew instinctively that they had taken over a superior civilization. So brute force doesn't necessitate cultural or intellectual superiority. If brute force were the only determinant of civilizational superiority, we would have to say that the Third Reich was superior to what it conquered. It's a foolish argument.

It is a historical fact that capitalism, having triumphed in Europe and gained technological superiority, began to educate its population, because this education was needed to run empires. But even at the time that the British took India, early British arrivals were amazed by the riches they found in Indian cities and how advanced these cities were. They were so shaken, in fact, by what they found—the culture of the land, the fact that the artisans in places like Dhaka and Delhi were so much superior to anything they had seen in Europe—that their first reaction was to loot the treasuries, to loot goods, to use force. The notion that they had conquered an inferior civilization is laughable, as is the notion that the countries who took parts of Shanghai and developed concessions and weakened that society were in some way superior to the civilization of China. Capitalism developed in Europe first, and that established a big technological advantage, which the Europeans used, naturally, to promote their own interests. But to say that European societies were superior is something I don't accept. They used their initial advantage to loot parts of the world, first via slavery, then through imperial conquest—that's how they built their empires, their societies, and their so-called superiority.

It's interesting that the word "loot" is of South Asian origin.

It is a Hindi and Urdu word, but it's become part of the English lexicon, thanks to the empire.

You were born in 1943. You came of age in a period of enormous ferment in the so-called Third World—it wasn't called the Third World then, of course—massive decolonization. There was the conference at Bandung, a city in central Java in Indonesia, where Nehru, Zhou Enlai, Sukarno, Nkrumah, Tito, and Nasser all gathered. There was a real sense of a new world developing, and there was a lot of excitement. What happened to that spirit of Bandung?

Decolonization was fresh, and there was a great deal of excitement. The populations in these countries were idealistic; they thought they could move forward, and the Bandung spirit—for Nehru and Nasser and Tito and Sukarno—represented a third way forward for the Third World, a real third way, not capitalist and not Communist in the Stalinist sense of the word. Sensibly, at that point, they didn't want to mimic the structures of the Soviet Union, and that's what created the excitement. The space for this existed only because the United States was not yet the only force in the world—the Soviet Union was still a superpower. The Chinese Revolution also gave enormous fillip to this movement: the world's largest country had undergone a major social upheaval, and the people ruling China were, in a broad sense, on our side. The conference at Bandung represented that spirit.

What happened to it? Many of these countries, even though they tried to keep out of the Cold War, were caught up in it. In Indonesia, which hosted the conference, there was a coup d'état ten years after Bandung, and the massacre of a million-plus Communists and their supporters, which created a massive vacuum in Indonesian society. Many of the killers, as I argue in *The Clash of Fundamentalisms,* were Islamic vigilantes, who then formed their own organizations and are still active today—when you have a vacuum, when you wipe out secular nationalists and Communists, sooner or later something will fill that vacuum. In Indonesia it was filled by various official and unofficial religious parties. I hold the empire responsible for what happened to Indonesia.

Look at what happened in the Middle East and how Nasser was defeated in 1967. Israel launched a preemptive strike against Egypt and Syria, and seized large new tracts of territory: it was a blow from which Nasser never recovered. He resigned immediately after the war, in one of the most moving episodes in Egyptian history: people all over the country poured onto the streets, like a river in flood, and said, Don't go; we are still with you. And he wept and stayed on.

But a few years later he was dead. Sadat replaced him and cut a deal with the Israelis to tie Egypt completely to the war chariot of the empire. And in order to destroy the influence of Nasserism and Leftism in Egypt, Sadat used Islamist vigilantes to go and clean out the universities; it was during his term that the Islamists began to acquire more and more influence. In the end, ironically, they finally dumped him as well.

You mentioned the 1965 coup in Indonesia, which brought General Suharto to power. The CIA supplied lists of suspected leftists to the Indonesian army, which hunted them down and killed them. It's interesting because there was an immediate precedent for that in 1963 in Iraq.

The CIA was ready to supply lists to anyone who was prepared to wipe out the Communists. In 1963, they gave names to the Iraqi Ba'ath, and King Hussein of Jordan confirmed this. As an old CIA agent, he knew. Mohamed Heikal, the Egyptian journalist and friend of Nasser, was taunting Hussein for making Jordan a virtual U.S. protectorate, and Hussein said in response, What are you talking about? What about the Iraqi Ba'ath—I know for a fact the CIA has supplied them with lists of Communists who are to be executed.

The person in charge of the Ba'ath internal security apparatus at that time was dear old Saddam Hussein, and this is when his close ties with American intelligence began—he always worked closely with the United States. He only became a so-called anti-imperialist after the Kuwait adventure failed, and even that he thought the United States had approved. Giving names to potential killers didn't start in Iraq and didn't end in Indonesia. In Latin America, not only were these lists supplied, U.S. intelligence agencies often participated in the actual torture and killing of Latin American oppositionists and real or potential guerrillas. Philip Agee's classic book *Inside the Company* recounts this story in some detail; it is what caused him to resign.

It's not over today—the enemies have just changed. Now it's not Communists they're after—now they hunt their old allies. What is happening in Guantánamo is only a modern version of the old process. The enemies have changed, but the methods remain the same.

You make a pun on the word Ba'ath, which means renais-
sance in Arabic—you say it was a "blood Ba'ath" in 1963. One
of the top Ba'athist leaders at the time—Ahmad al-Bakr—said
"We rode to power on the U.S. locomotive."

They knew perfectly well how they had taken power.
The choice confronting the United States at the time was
to support the Ba'ath or possibly see the Iraqi Communist
Party take power through a popular insurrection, so they
decided to go for the Ba'ath. Without American support,
it's an open question what would have happened; we don't
know and it would be foolish to speculate. Today, when
the Ba'ath is demonized, people must be reminded of
these facts. Don't forget the history: The Ba'ath Party
began as a nationalist party, and the Iraqi wing made a deal
with the United States. Syrian Ba'athists attacked the
Iraqis over this, accusing them of caving in to the Americans; the Iraqi Ba'athists' open capitulation to the needs of
the American intelligence services was one cause of the
hostility between Syria and Iraq. This collaboration suited
the interests of the Iraqi Ba'ath—they weren't just
stooges; it helped them tremendously.

Is there solid evidence that King Hussein was a CIA agent?

It would be an exaggeration to call him an "agent."
He wasn't on their payroll or working directly for them.

But he was very close to the CIA, and the fact of his collaboration is beyond dispute. He crushed the Palestinian
uprising in September 1970, which both the Israelis and
the U.S. asked him to do. They thought that the Palestinian camps in Jordan were a threat to Hussein and to them.
A majority of the population is Palestinian, and a large
part of Jordan was Palestine anyway. Parts of Palestine
had been sold to the Zionists by Hussein's father, King
Abdullah, who was killed as a result; this is a collaboration that goes back a long way. Hussein decided that the
only way he could survive as king of Jordan—not the only
way Jordan could survive, the only way *he* could
survive—was by making Jordan into an American-Israeli
protectorate, which he did and which it remains to
this day.

The key turning point was Black September, in
1970, when he decided to crush the Palestinians. Inter-
estingly enough, the Pakistani brigadier chosen to help
them was Zia ul-Haq, the so-called friend of Islam, who
was dispatched by the Pakistani government. Zia organized the massacre of the Palestinians, for which the
Palestinians never forgave him. I have in my archives a
very striking photograph, of a celebration in a Jordanian
army mess after the crushing of the Palestinian camps
and the resistance in Jordan. Brigadier Zia and one of
Hussein's officers are dancing; the Jordanian is clearly
drunk, and whether Zia had had one or two remains
an open question. Later, of course, he masqueraded as a

devout Muslim, but I never forgot that episode in Palestine.

I said to Benazir Bhutto, "This man is going to topple your father. He is the Uriah Heep of Pakistani politics. In front of you he sort of cringes and is servile and sycophantic, but in his head there is another plan." I said this after I returned from Pakistan in January 1977, after I had a few clashes with Benazir's father, Zulfikar Ali Bhutto. She was then at the Oxford Union and invited me to speak. She said to me, "My father rang me today and asked me, 'Why are you inviting my enemies to speak?' " "He's always been very childish and stupid," I replied, and she said, "I know. But my father said to me, 'Now that you've got him there, ask him what he thinks is going to happen in Pakistan.' " I said—I'll never forget this conversation—"Tell your father from me that either he will be assassinated or there will be a military coup." And she said, "Assassinations, who can stop them? A military coup, never, because General Zia is in our pocket," and she touched her imaginary pocket. I said, "Benazir, you just tell your father I said that no Pakistani general is ever in the pocket of a civilian politician." Three months later, General Zia carried out his coup, and Bhutto lost his job and later his life.

Almost parallel to that Bandung spirit in the 1950s, there was a tremendous amount of writing coming out of the postcolonial world. It was perhaps preceded a bit earlier by C.L.R. James, the Trinidadian author of The Black Jacobins. *But then you had Frantz Fanon, Aimé Césaire, and Amilcar Cabral. Who are the anti-imperialist theorists today that people should be reading?*

To your list I would add the Indonesian writer Pramoedya Ananta Toer, who wrote some wonderful fiction and nonfiction, and was locked up in really bad prison conditions by the Indonesian generals for most of his life. He's still alive, in fact: Pramoedya Ananta Toer deserves the Nobel Prize for Literature, if anyone does, but I find it interesting who does and does not get considered for the Nobel—the committee always has one eye on the needs of the establishment. Since the collapse of the Soviet Union, for example, no Russian has gotten the Nobel Prize for Literature. In Pakistan, we had poets like Faiz Ahmed Faiz, and in India, a vast number of writers. Who are the anti-imperialist theorists of today? In that world it's very difficult to find people of the caliber of those you mentioned.

Why is that?

There was a great demoralization after the collapse of the anticolonial movements and following the final triumph of capitalism in 1989. The intelligentsia in that part of the world went into retreat. This has not been entirely the case in the Arab world, but there it was not intellectuals like Cabral, Césaire, Fanon, or Toer who took over the reins—it was the Arab poets who became the voices of their nations, as we discussed earlier. Nizar Qabbani, Saadi Youssef, Mudhaffar al-Nawab—all these poets played a similar role to the one played by intellectuals in the 1940s and 1950s, in the early colonial and postcolonial period.

We have talked about poets, but let's consider the great bard of empire—the pied piper of British imperialism, Rudyard Kipling, who coined the term "white man's burden." His evolution is very interesting: He lost his son in World War I, and then wrote "Epitaphs of the War." Let me read you a couple of the lines: "If any question why we died, Tell them, because our fathers lied." In another poem, titled "A Dead Statesman," he wrote:

I could not dig: I dared not rob:
Therefore I lied to please the mob.
Now all my lies are proved untrue
And I must face the men I slew.
What tale shall serve me here among
Mine angry and defrauded young?

Very beautiful lines—and very relevant to the war in Iraq, to the young men and women Blair and Bush decided to send to their death, to the young Iraqis and old Iraqis, ten thousand of them, who have been killed. I love that poem by Kipling, and in fact I used it in one of my speeches in the run-up to the war. Kipling was a very

strange guy: he was from a ruling-class British family—
he was related to Stanley Baldwin, the prime minister of
Britain, a very underestimated prime minister of Britain,
at a critical stage for the empire. There is no doubt that
Kipling was a bard of the empire. There's a wonderful
poem by Bertolt Brecht about Kipling. Brecht, like many
of us, disliked Kipling's politics, but at the same time,
couldn't help admiring his verses.

Kind of like Naipaul.

Indeed, very similar to Naipaul. There is a wonderful
poem by Brecht about the deaths in the First World War.
He talks about the last days of Queen Victoria, and he says
in his refrain:

> *"Oh, East is East and West is West!"*
> *Their hireling minstrel cried.*
> *But I observed with interest*
> *Bridges across that great divide*
> *And huge guns trundling East I've seen*
> *And cheerful troops keeping them clean.*
> *Meanwhile, from east to west, back rolled*
> *Tea soaked in blood, war wounded, gold*

It's a wonderful poem. Brecht translated a number of
Kipling's poems into German and used them as songs in
his plays.

Kipling is interesting—he may be the only "imperial" novelist who couldn't help being at the same time very critical of aspects of empire. He was the only British writer at the height of the empire who could capture and convey the accents of ordinary English working people: he was the bard of the Tommies in India; he spoke for them as well. The upper crust of the empire in India, therefore, did not like much of Kipling's work—not because he was pro-Indian but because he was an advocate for the lower-class English people who were forced to serve the needs of the empire.

That poem you read has a history itself: I think Kipling knew that he was to blame for his son's death—it was not just the politicians who lied. Kipling's son had very bad eyesight, which would have prevented him from being drafted into the army, but Kipling used his position in British society—pulled rank, as they say—to make sure that his son's disability was ignored and he could enter the army. He died in battle not long after enlisting, and one of his fellow soldiers said he was killed because his glasses had fallen off and he couldn't see. When Kipling heard this, of course, he was devastated; that poem expresses Kipling's bitterness and anger with himself—he knew that jingoism had driven him to send his own son to die.

In "On the Road to Mandalay"—one of Kipling's most famous poems—he writes, "Ship me somewhere east of Suez, where

the best is like the worst, / Where there aren't no Ten Command-
ments an' a man can raise a thirst." It conjures up a whole notion
of the East as a kind of terra nullius, *either an empty land or*
just a place of great sensuality, where the white man could go
forth and have women and treasures and magic lamps and flying
carpets.

We can see this Orientalist exotica at work; that was
the only world they could see, because they never looked
any deeper. Kipling, to be fair, did, but most didn't. There
were not only women to be had but, we mustn't forget
this, also men. Boys of every age were readily available in
that world—it was not regarded as something scan-
dalous. In some of Kipling's short stories, we can see
where his interests totally dovetail with those of the empire: he portrays the Bengali, for example, as a short,
dark, permanent talker with the mentality of a clerk,
babu. The British were very threatened by the Bengalis,
because the Bengalis picked up the English language very
quickly, learned a great deal, and produced an intelligentsia which challenged the empire before any other
part of India. Raja Ram Mohan Roy, the Hindu reformer,
used to say, "What Bengal thinks today, India thinks tomorrow."

The intellectual Bengali, who asks too many questions, thinks too much, and talks too much—which they
resented—was counterposed with the beauty of the mar-
tial races: the Punjabi Jat peasant fighter, and of course the

Pathan, descended from the tribes of Alexander the Great, the six-foot-tall men of fair skin, often with red hair and blue eyes, who peopled the Northwest Frontier of India—where homosexuality was part of everyday life. Bisexuality, one should say—boys for pleasure and women for procreation. Kipling and lots of other English administrators fell for that. I've always wondered—I don't know whether there is any evidence for this— whether Kipling himself was bisexual, because some of the emotional intensity in those short stories is quite staggering; it is almost as if he had had an affair with someone. It's like the character Ronald Merrick, in Paul Scott's *The Raj Quartet,* who is both repulsed and attracted to India.

One of Edward Said's favorite novelists was the Polish-born Joseph Conrad, the author of Heart of Darkness—*later to became the basis for Francis Ford Coppola's* Apocalypse Now. *Listen to a couple of lines from* Heart of Darkness. *He was familiar with what the Belgians were doing in the Congo and what else was going on in Africa—the enormous carnage. He describes London, in the opening lines, as "the greatest town on earth." His character Marlowe is sitting in the* Nellie, *this boat anchored in the Thames. At the same time, he says it's also "one of the dark places of the earth."*

Conrad was always an outsider in British culture. This duality existed in Conrad's person: he was a Pole, a sailor, who learned English at a late stage and then mastered the language. Much like Isaac Deutscher, also a Pole, and a Marxist, did many years later—Deutscher had no English when he fled Poland as a refugee. I always think of Deutscher and Conrad together: very different people, in very different times; both Poles who became masterly writers of English prose. Deutscher's three-volume biography of Trotsky, politics aside, is beautifully written, and Conrad's writings are equally stunning. What makes them stunning is precisely the fact that they are not English—their way of writing English is very special. And, of course, Conrad found London, like William Blake before him, a city with very dark corners: these were the cities of colonial trade, of plunder, of imperial might, and this had an effect on people inside the metropolis.

I had to read *The Secret Agent* when I was still at school—it was one of our textbooks, and the first book of Conrad's I read. It has a funny side to it, but at the same time, there is another reading of it: Why are these anarchists holed up in there? Why are they doing what they're doing? That's a reading that no one wants to make, and Conrad always embodied this duality. One sentence in *Heart of Darkness* has probably become one of the most powerful lines in modern literature: "The horror! The horror!" Conrad was writing about the Congo, which King Leopold essentially owned as a personal colony; it was later transferred to Belgium, but initially it was the property of the Belgian king. Conrad described the brutality of colonialism in the Congo, and in that he was not alone: As we've discussed, Sir Arthur Conan Doyle, who came from a very different background, was also obsessed with the Congo; his book on the atrocities was a tremendous bestseller.

Adam Hochschild's wonderful book *King Leopold's Ghost* recounts all of this—it is a very valuable addition to world history and our knowledge of empires. The figures Hochschild provides—that between ten and twelve million Congolese died—confirm the scale of the atrocities; this was the biggest massacre of the twentieth century, though it began at the end of the previous century. The predecessor to the Judeocide of the Second World War, which wiped out six million Jews, was the murder of twelve million Africans earlier in the century. We have to put all these things into context.

It was Kurtz in Heart of Darkness *who says those words, "The horror! The horror!"*

Kurtz is portrayed as a weird, strange, crazed man. But even he sees "The horror! The horror!" in which he has himself partially participated. Coppola makes Marlon Brando the Kurtz figure in Vietnam, which I thought was the weakest part of that film. The first three-quarters of *Apocalypse Now* is a powerful antiwar statement, but then he goes down this mystical track with Brando and the mountain tribes of Vietnam—pure mysticism, based on nothing save the fact that the empire used those tribes. To me that didn't work; it actually weakened the film.

In Heart of Darkness, *Conrad writes, "They were conquerors, and for that you only want brute force. . . . It was just robbery with violence, aggravated murder on a grand scale, and men going at it blind. . . . The conquest of the earth, which mostly means the taking it away from those who have a different complexion or slightly flatter noses than ourselves, is not a pretty thing when you look into it too much. What redeems it is the idea only." At that time, of course, it was the white man's burden,* la mission civilitrice, *manifest destiny. Perhaps today the idea is the axis of evil, the war on terrorism, humanitarian interventions. Talk about the new lexicon of imperialism—you're a critic of the American and British intervention in the Balkans.*

As the Cold War recedes into the past, a number of analysts of empire are beginning to see the continuities between the Balkan wars and Iraq, which certainly exist. What is curious is that all this talk of humanitarian intervention was taken quite seriously by the citizens of Europe and North America. They genuinely wanted to believe that their governments had gone in to do good, and because they wanted to believe it, they did; they couldn't see any other side to it at all. As we said at the time, if they wanted to do good, why did they intervene in the Balkans and not in Rwanda, where a real genocide was taking place, where a UN intervention would have saved tens of thousands of Tutsis? When Boutros Boutros-Ghali, the last slightly independent-minded secretary-general of the UN, raised this point, the Clinton administration replaced him with Kofi Annan, who wholeheartedly supported intervention in the Balkans while murders of the worst sort were taking place in Rwanda, on his own continent.

This is why the Americans and British tried to suggest that what was happening in the Balkans was genocide—because they knew a real genocide was taking place in Rwanda, whereas what was happening in the Balkans was an unpleasant, nasty, ugly civil war, provoked by a partition of Yugoslavia that had been backed by the European powers, in particular by the Germans, who bear heavy responsibility for what happened there. Once you decide to partition a country, populations have to be moved or they flee out of fear—as we saw in India and Pakistan in 1947, it becomes very ugly. Demonizing one side or the other is not very helpful when people on all sides are dying. This was a decision taken by the German foreign office, to detach Slovenia and Croatia. Milosevic didn't help, of course, and one can't absolve him of blame. His ultra-nationalism and that of Radovan Karadic and that of Tudjman of Croatia led to terrible crimes being committed in Bosnia. The massacre in Srebrenica is unforgettable and unforgivable as was the destruction of Mostar and the expulsion of the Krajina Serbs. But the Europeans used Balkan weakness to divide up that territory, with disastrous results. We now have two UN–U.S. protectorates, in Bosnia and Kosovo, where life has not improved—it remains miserable. What was finally achieved? The humanitarian interventionists no longer talk about Bosnia or Kosovo; they've lost interest and moved on.

In his book *The Shield of Achilles,* Philip Bobbitt, who was on Clinton's National Security Council, says there is a total continuity between Clinton and Bush; he takes a lot of credit for intervening in the Balkans, because American interests, according to Bobbitt, were directly served there. We now have bases there, and we managed to expand NATO. The Balkan war was a war to expand NATO, to show that NATO had a role to play, and to encircle Russia, and it succeeded. It completely weakened Russia as a world power—that was the basic function of the U.S. intervention; it had nothing to do with humanitarian aims. It's interesting that some of the humanitarian interventionists were opposed to the war in Iraq. Why? You could use exactly the same arguments. But I think they had begun to wear a bit thin. It was, of course, completely naive of these people to imagine that empires act for anything but their own interests.

Let's talk about one of the cracks in the edifice of empire, Argentina. Quite an exceptional country in many ways: a high literacy rate, a sophisticated and trained workforce, rich in natural resources. It was the poster boy for neoliberalism. It strictly fol-

*lowed World Bank and IMF nostrums, and it has undergone one
of the greatest economic collapses of any country in history.*

Argentina saw itself as a kind of Europe in Latin
America: This was a country where the native population
had been virtually exterminated. In Charles Darwin's di-
aries, he recounts arriving in Argentina during his long
tour of the world to write *The Origin of Species* and being
shocked by the massacres taking place there. This is a man
who is discovering the science of evolution, and here he
sees before his eyes that humans are replicating the behavior of the animals, wiping out the native population.
Argentina is the only country in Latin America where the
natives were entirely eliminated. And then they peopled
the country with migrants from Europe, Italians largely,
but also Spaniards and others.

There is a wonderful book by Domingo Sarmiento,
who later became president of Argentina, called *Facundo,*
which gives an account of the civil wars that wrecked Argentina, the clashes that took place, and the barbarism
that Argentines deployed, not just against the natives, but
against one another, to create this so-called Europe in
Latin America. Sarmiento's book, written in the nineteenth century, describes the divide between two ten-
dencies, the gauchos and the Europeans. The European
influence is said to be civilizing, while the gauchos represent native barbarism. It's quite an interesting book, very
beautifully written.

Argentina and its enlightened liberals saw themselves as no different from Europe; if you go to Buenos Aires, you will see it's constructed on the model of a European city: it's a wonderful city, with parks and large avenues. There was, certainly, a narcissism in Argentina, which thought itself better than the rest of Latin America. It wasn't laid out explicitly, rationalized, or explained, but this is what they believed. For Argentines of all social classes—from the bottom up and from the top down—the collapse of their economy was a psychological disaster.

I visited Argentina during this period, and some friends said to me, "We are going to show you something which has never happened in this country before, but you have to stay up until midnight." We went to a café, and at midnight we walked back to my hotel, and we saw hordes of kids from the suburbs who had come into the center of Buenos Aires with gloves on—it was all well organized—to empty the trash bins and filter the garbage in them. "This," my friends said, "we have never seen in Argentina before."

This is a country whose leaders systematically followed the advice of the IMF, the World Bank, and the United States Treasury Department, which used to intervene regularly—a country that collapsed. It was a collapse of neoliberal economics, and it was a real flowering of democracy—local democracy on every level. I attended one of the popular assemblies in Buenos Aires—

towards the end of their prominence, it has to be said. But there were dozens of these committees in every quarter of Buenos Aires—local people coming together to discuss the future of their country.

Here is the real tragedy: there were lots of popular initiatives, but there was no existing overall alternative to the neoliberal economic system for Argentina. This is something many of the theorists of the World Social Forum underestimate. True, Argentina collapsed, and Nestor Kirchner, a Peronist of sorts, is president. But what happened to the grassroots movements? What happened to its leaders? Why didn't they come up with an alternative? Many of them said, We don't want to come up with a political alternative. This is fatal, because if you do not produce a political alternative, the same system returns again. I said to an Argentinian friend, There is a fear of using the *S* word—"socialism"—again, and this is foolish. We have to popularize it again, because this remains the only alternative. Obviously, one must learn from all the mistakes and not repeat them. How come capitalism has failed dozens of times in its history, and it comes back again and again? Socialism failed only once, and we're not going to be given another chance?

We have to develop ideas of a noncapitalist economy, a socialist economy—which means heavy state intervention—and try to create a different system, in which people function on every level. Not a system like the Soviet Union, but one that is socialist and more dem-

ocratic than capitalism today: capitalist democracy is on
the decline, without any doubt, because there are no economic alternatives permitted within it. Argentina, from
that point of view, is very revealing: it demonstrates the
failures of neoliberal economics and the Washington consensus, but also the weakness of the alternative.

*But there have also been instances, since the economic
collapse, of Argentinian workers organizing, taking over
workplaces—that kind of collective action.*

These were very important at the time, and the ability of the workers to organize themselves showed, as we
have always known, that workers and working people are
completely capable of taking their destiny into their own
hands. But if these initiatives remain local, they can't
work for very long. It's exemplary, it offers a model, and
it proves that a different future is possible, but unless it's
systematized and done on a national scale, it's not going
to work.

Many people said, "We don't want to think along the
lines of states and borders." But the nation-state has not
disappeared—it's still there, and it offers possibilities.
This utopian notion that globalized capitalism has dis-
solved boundaries so we should dissolve them as well is
nonsense. Globalized capitalism needs a nation-state to
push through its plans; it needs a state, and the alternative
needs a state, too. Instead of rejecting the state, I think ac-

tivists and their movements have to figure out how to take over the state. This was common sense in my generation, but it sounds shocking today; it still has to be done, but done differently. The slogan "We can change the world without taking state power" is touching for its naivety, but any strategy and tactics that flow out of it can only be self-defeating.

For more years than you would probably like to remember, you've been speaking at conferences on "The Crisis in Capitalism." What gives the system its resilience? Consider the crisis in Argentina: They float more loans, they throw more money at the country, they print more money, and it's patched over and they go on.

It will continue to go on unless there is an alternative. The only time in its history that capitalism was forced to make massive concessions to working people, both in terms of democratic rights, the right to form trade unions, and social reforms, was when another enemy appeared on the horizon. This enemy wasn't a religious enemy—it promised a social vision far superior and more equal than anything possible under capitalism. This was the world envisaged in *The Communist Manifesto.* That experiment failed, but the question is, Did it have to fail? I would say no. If the leaders of the Russian Revolution and the second generation had understood that the way in which the state took over everything was completely wrong, if they had permitted petty commodity production and not stupidly prevented people from opening their own restaurants and things like that, while at the same time keeping the commanding heights of the economy under a form of democratic state control, encouraging workers to play a part in managing industry and maintaining a democratic political structure, this system would have spread. It would not have been defeated in the way that it was.

We always used to say to supporters of the Soviet model, "How come a capitalist system can exist alongside a multiparty democracy? What is it that prevents a multiparty democracy in your system?" For this they had no answer—they could only claim, falsely, that Western democracy was fake. But the multiparty system in the West, for all its weaknesses—and they're much more pronounced in the United States—offers a mechanism, a transmission belt for incorporating some consent of ordinary people into the system. The Soviets had no mechanism save for force, repression, or censorship. This was a fatal flaw in the Soviet system that led to its downfall. When a new socialism emerges, it must be more democratic than what exists today; otherwise, it's not going to work.

Gore Vidal calls America the United States of Amnesia. Few Americans know that shortly after the revolution, the Soviet Union was invaded by the European powers, the United States, and Japan. That invasion surely had a deleterious effect on the

possibility that the revolution might develop into a more demo-
cratic form. It hardened the hardliners, who said, "Look, we're
surrounded—our enemies are attacking us."

About fifteen or sixteen foreign armies intervened
to try and crush this revolution; it's always thus. All the
monarchies in Europe came together in a holy alliance to
try to defeat the French Revolution—war was waged on
revolutionary France. The same thing happened to revolutionary Russia. The attempt to destroy the revolution
led to a ferocious civil war in Russia, in which the cream
of the Soviet working class lost their lives. Large numbers
of the most political workers, who had made the revolution, died in the war, which meant that the armory of the
revolution, in human terms, was depleted. That enabled
the development of bureaucracy, bureaucratization, the
victory of Stalin, and the emergence of Stalinism as a political system.

If the revolution had been allowed to develop freely,
who knows where it would have gone? There were other
parties, after all, like the Mensheviks, who were not
against the revolution and would have worked within it as
a loyal opposition. These parties and their presses were
all banned during the civil war, when Lenin said, "Our
survival is at risk. Nothing else matters. We have to crush
all enemies." Had there not been an intervention and
open attempts by the Americans, and particularly by
Churchill, to back the White Russians in the civil war,

none of this would have taken place. Russia had already been drained by the First World War, in which nearly two million of its people died, and then, on top of that, a civil war—this created awful conditions in which to build socialism or anything approaching democratic socialism.

It's a great tragedy; if a democratic socialism had emerged in the Soviet Union, it would have had a real effect on China, Cuba, and Vietnam. The United States and the West waged an ideological offensive against socialism on the grounds that it was not democratic—and to that, there was no answer. There is a famous story from Antonio Gramsci's tenure as a Communist deputy in the Italian parliament: Mussolini banned trade unions, and when Gramsci stood up to attack him, Mussolini said, "Why are you complaining when the same thing is happening in your beloved Soviet Union?" Gramsci tried to reply, but there was not much he could say.

There is evidence that elites inside the United States, at the Council on Foreign Relations, and in other centers of power are quite disturbed by the extreme actions of the Bush administration. It would not be surprising if there were regime change in this country in November. But, again, the empire has this ability to change its clothes and put a new emperor on the throne.

There is no doubt that serious forces within the American ruling class are perturbed by this administration. In the days of the Roman Empire, if the senate realized that the emperor was completely unusable, they went and murdered him. In the United States, of course, you can't do that, or at least the senate can't do that, so they remove him from power.

What if he loses—what will that mean? First, there is no doubt in my mind that the whole world will rejoice if Bush is defeated. It will be seen as a victory for the peace movement, which can say, "This is the guy who went to war, and now he's been punished by his electors." There will be celebratory gatherings all over the world—it will be seen as a defeat, and rightly so—for Bush's particular politics.

However, as I argued during the run-up to the war in Iraq, if a war in Iraq is wrong because it's carried out unilaterally by the United States, is it right if it is conducted under the banner of the United Nations? I see absolutely no logic in that at all. A Democratic president will revert to Clinton-type imperial rule, where you make sure these wretched Europeans are on board so they don't kick up a fuss. Help them, share the loot with them, give them a bit of the oil, give them a bit of the contracts in Iraq, and get them on board. Bush himself is beginning to embrace this approach—he told the Canadians, who opposed the war and refused to send troops in, Don't worry, we'll give you some contracts, and sent Donald Rumsfeld to weep tears over his memories of the Korean War at Munich.

Bush has begun this process, but because his credibility is very low, the people who will take it forward—if they win—will be the Democrats. Even if they don't win, I think the neocon period in American history might be over—even a new Bush regime would probably transform itself into a more benign-looking empire. That's certainly what the Democrats will do. One shouldn't have any illusions that a Democratic victory is going to mean the end of empire; far from it.

You've been projecting the emergence of a cluster of nations in the Far East, around China, Japan, and Korea, as a potential countervailing force to U.S. power. These are state capitalist regimes—certainly no alternative. Is it going to be a replication of the rise of German state capitalism contesting with the British, which is what happened in the First World War and the Second World War?

I would not suggest that the Far Eastern bloc represents the kind of alternative we've been discussing—an alternative to capitalism. However, the emergence of a Far Eastern bloc could represent a very significant rival—the only serious one—to the American empire. If inter-imperialist contradictions begin to develop, my feeling is that the clash will come not between Europe and America but between the Far Eastern bloc and the United States, which might subsequently give the Europeans sufficient courage to become a power in their own right. They will certainly not do it on their own.

All of this would just return us to what has been the status quo during previous phases of imperialist rule—the situation at the moment, where there is only one imperial power, is unique in human history. The prospect of these other powers emerging is what leads the United States to maintain its bases in Okinawa and refuse to withdraw troops from Korea. If Korea becomes unified, why station U.S. troops there? Why are there U.S. military bases in Okinawa? Their only function is to prevent the Japanese from having their own foreign policy, to draw them increasingly into the American net; this is why Koizumi has been forced to send a contingent of Japanese troops to Iraq. Can you imagine? There is a contingent of Japanese soldiers policing tiny bits of Iraq. All of this prevents any progress toward the emergence of a Far Eastern bloc, which would certainly be in the interests of Chinese, Japanese, and Korean capitalism. It would be best for them to have their own union, a big regional bloc, but the United States is determined to stop that.

Until now, the United States has been content to apply pressure to prevent this union—but would they consider using force to stop a Far Eastern bloc from emerging? Will they do something truly reckless, such as attempting to balkanize China? They could foment unrest in either Tibet or Taiwan, I suppose—those are the alternatives available to the Americans. But Tibet now is on the verge of a settlement with the Beijing regime. The Dalai Lama, apparently, has suggested that as long as Tibet has autonomy, he is not worried about leaving China. He wants the Chinese to carry on running foreign policy and defense policy, and those are their big concerns. If this is true, Taiwan remains the only instrument the United States has in the region, and what happens there will be crucial. This is how we must view the region, through the lens of this union, which the United States is trying to prevent; they can see that this is the real competition to their empire.

You did not mention Muslim western China.

The Chinese are nervous about western China, but the people who are creating mayhem there are the same people who are making trouble for the United States elsewhere—the Afghan war veterans. Men from western China went to Afghanistan to join the *jihad* against the Soviets, and now they've returned to create problems at home. The Chinese, of course, have dealt with this in a brutal and vicious fashion, and they have the region under control. The only place where the Americans can create mischief is Taiwan—if the Taiwanese are willing, which is an open question. The Beijing regime should propose a Chinese commonwealth to all the Chinese territories and abandon their claim to Taiwan if they have to. Once Taiwan and China have access to each other's markets, it will be very difficult for Taiwan to be used by the Americans as a military base to destabilize the mainland. It is in the interest of Beijing to make a deal.

Explain the rule of the BJP [Bharatiya Janata Party] in India and the rise of Hindu fundamentalism. We've mentioned the massacre in Gujarat in 2002, which was preceded by another pogrom in Bombay in 1992. There has been a history of communal violence on the Indian subcontinent.

Hindu fundamentalism is the first serious attempt to create a Hindu nationalism in India in the modern period. The old nationalist leaders like Nehru and Gandhi were composite nationalists: Gandhi invoked Hindu imagery, but he talked about India as a united nation of many different peoples and actually gave up his life defending Muslims who were being massacred soon after partition. Now Indian nationalism has been replaced by Hindu nationalism, at least to a large extent; in that, the BJP has been instrumental. The collapse of the only existing social alternatives to capitalism—communism and socialism—has created a great vacuum, and this vacuum has been filled by people who say, "In the world today every man must fend for himself. We must fight for our identities, because this is a competitive world. Our identity is that of a Hindu nation, and all the others, especially the Muslim minority, do not matter." The circumstances are quite similar to those that gave rise to increased religious fundamentalism in the Muslim world, in the United States, in Israel, and all over the world. In India, the social safety nets, which the Nehru Congress had kept in place, have been abandoned, and the situation at the lower rungs of society has only worsened. It's this competition that encourages the use of Muslims as scapegoats. Poor Hindus look derisively at these Muslims who are just as poor, if not worse. But the poor Hindus can be mobilized against the Muslims, to loot their houses, wipe them out, rape their wives, beat up their children. This has happened systematically, and culminated in Gujarat.

The shocking thing is that the government in Gujarat, which supervised and presided over the massacres, was reelected. The Congress Party proved completely incapable of offering an alternative. The candidate they put up against Narendra Modi, the chief minister of Gujarat, was someone who had defected from the BJP to the Congress—what a joke. In the old days, the Dalits, the so-called untouchable caste, and their leader, B.R. Ambedkar, used to say, "We don't want to be classified as Hindus. Hindus are Brahmans. We are not." But no one, not even Gandhi, would agree to that, because the proportion of Hindus in the population would decline if you left out the lower castes. The BJP, sadly, which was essentially an upper-class and middle-class party, is now beginning to win support from the Hindu lower castes. This is worrying, but I think it reflects the world in which we live.

Narendra Modi was implicated in the 2002 pogrom in Gujarat.

His police force watched people being massacred, Muslim houses being burnt to the ground, women being raped, and he did not act. One of the most horrific aspects of the violence was the total failure of the state to protect one segment of the population from another. Modi defended his police force and refused to believe these allegations—he announced publicly they were false. Now that he has been reelected, he's totally out of control.

Let me just ask you, finally, about yourself. How do you keep hope alive? How do you keep those inner fires burning?

I try not to think about it—the last person I think about is myself. I've never been a person tempted by power, either in the world or in the academy; it's never interested me. I have no desire to be a professor. I don't mean that there aren't good professors, but I've never been attracted to that life. I've always lived and earned my living as an independent writer, and I carry on doing it. I never thought I would be writing nonfiction again, but since September 11, I've felt forced to write these books. When readers in Germany or Brazil or Spain berate me for not completing the "Islam Quintet," I say, "Blame Bush."

This has in turn led to a great deal of traveling, all over the world; I get maybe thirty or forty invitations each week, from every continent. I can't do them all, of course, but neither can I do none—that would be a total abdication of one's responsibility as a vigilant and alert citizen. I go where I can. I travel to the United States a great deal—I get more invitations from the United States than anywhere else. I try to accept as many of them as possible, precisely because I think that this country is crucial—its public opinion is crucial to the future, because it can have some countervailing pressure on the American ruling class, and perhaps change the world.

There are a handful of us, globally, doing this sort of thing, and I'm absolutely desperate for a new generation of people to emerge and take over, because the weight that falls on you, the pressure to do things, is sometimes a bit frightening. If you turn down invitations, people say, "Oh, you're getting too big for your boots." But I'm sixty years old now, and at this age I do as much as I can. I've now developed the art of doing a lot of work on the long plane journeys to the West Coast, the East Coast, to Australia, and New Zealand.

The critical thing for me is that my fiction project—which dear Edward Said forced me on many, many years ago—remains unfinished. After *Shadows of the Pomegranate Tree,* an account of the fall of Islamic civilization in Spain, was published, Edward read the book and liked it. He said, "You can't just stop now. You must carry on and tell the whole story, because this is just the beginning." So then I wrote *The Book of Saladin,* about the Crusades, the reconquest of Jerusalem by the Arabs and the Jews, and the driving out of the Crusaders. It is the only novel of mine to be translated into Hebrew by an Israeli publisher, because it shows the links between Muslims and Jews, which pleases me greatly. The third novel in that quintet is *The Stone Woman,* which depicts the Ottoman Empire and its decline and fall. I have two more novels to complete. The next one, *A Sultan in Palermo,* is set in twelfth-century Sicily because, while the history of the Crusades and of Islamic Spain is better known, Sicily is one of the least-known stories of Muslim rule and defeat in Europe. Palermo used to be called the city of a hundred mosques, and there is no trace of them left now; I'm going to reconstruct the period just after the Muslim defeat. The last of the novels will take place in the twentieth and twenty-first centuries, during present times, in which, I promise you, we'll have a lot of fun with the house Arabs and their chums.

7

Palestine and Israel

Explain why Palestine is so central to Muslim consciousness.

The question of Palestine evokes anger, despair, sadness, and bitterness because it was a very important part of the Arab world. The Palestinians were regarded as amongst the oldest inhabitants of that world. The crude, brutal way in which the state of Israel was created, with mass expulsions of Palestinians, the destruction of Palestinian villages, ethnic cleansing, the rape of Palestinian women—the exact numbers of which are yet to be revealed—left its mark on the Arab world. It was in some ways as much of a cultural and political shock as the entry of the Crusaders in the eleventh century had been. The nature of the shock was exactly the same: we had been violated, our world entered and taken away from us, and a

This interview, conducted in April 2004, has not previously been broadcast or published.

new state created in its place—without our permission, without collaboration, without discussion—by a major imperial power—Great Britain. That's what most Arab people thought.

To that shock can be added the total failure of the Arab armies to take back the territory, the fact that the armies were under the control of corrupt kings and officers who sabotaged the 1948 war. The Arab defeat was not merely due to Israeli superiority or Israeli fanaticism—which were there—it was a deliberate failure on the part of the Arab elites, who did not really want to win the war but needed to make a show of it. The depth of this shock is illustrated in the work of one of the greatest Arab writers of the twentieth century, Abdelrahman Munif—in his book *Story of a City: A Childhood in Amman,* where he describes the importance of Palestine, even to young children. Munif recounts that at school, when the teachers in class used to say, Name ten Arab cities, the first six names were always those of Palestinian cities, which are still with us today, in the news every single day. This failure went very deep. It was this failure that led to the birth of Arab nationalism. The establishment of Israel in the Arab world created a new wave of radical Arab nationalism, whose principal leader, Gamal Abdel Nasser, became probably the most popular leader in the Arab world since Saladin.

Since then we have seen the systematic crushing of the Palestinians; the wars waged, beginning with the

1967 war; and the continuing expansion of Israel's frontiers. The Zionist leadership attempted to wipe out the
Palestinians as a political force, to crush their spirit so
that they would forget who they once were. Like the
slaves who were once brought to the United States, they
hoped that these people, too, would develop new identities, new personas, and forget the past. But that failed
miserably and led us to the situation we are in today,
where every single attempt by the Palestinians to make
concessions in order to get something has collapsed.

Today we are here in the United States of America
discussing Israel and Palestine at a time when George
Bush has given the Israelis the green light to take whole
chunks of Palestine—he says it is utopian to return to the
1967 borders, that the settlers should remain, and that
Gaza should be turned into a prison camp, a large ghetto,
like the Warsaw ghetto, permanently supervised by Israel. In this situation, what can one say? It is, therefore,
unsurprising that Palestine remains central in the minds
of large numbers of Arab people, if not the corrupt, venal
elites who rule that world.

Given the daily breach of all human rights laws and
the daily violations of elementary human decency, why is
the liberal conscience of the West blind to Palestinian suffering? It is because, in the United States in particular, the
Palestinians as a people are widely regarded as terrorists,
to a person. This term is now used to describe anything
that opposes imperial interests or the interests of impe-

rial satrapies, and the Palestinians have been given this image in the mainstream American media. The liberals here are incredibly weak on this subject—in the United States, the world's dominant power, public opinion follows whatever the government says regarding the Palestinians: they're *Untermenschen,* they're subhuman; they're terrorists.

The degree of anti-Palestinian and anti-Arab racism is deeply shocking. If you compare what has been done to the Palestinians with what Milosevic did to the Kosovars, the crimes being committed in Palestine are of a totally different nature. Every single day the Israel Defense Forces, as they call it, targets children—young boys in particular. During the last three years, a week has rarely passed without the deaths of young boys in Palestine. This is approaching, not in terms of scale but in terms of intent, a genocidal war, to try and wipe out future generations of Palestinians. They justify it, disgustingly, by saying, We're destroying the terrorist bombers of tomorrow.

If the United States is blind to this, the Europeans are partially blind as well. They know what's going on and they are unhappy about it, but the Israelis have got them in a bind. The Germans are unwilling to speak against Israel because of the Judeocide of the Second World War. But the present generation of Germans is not responsible for that any more than the present generation of Belgians is responsible for the atrocities and genocide in the

Congo. You cannot make guilt retrospective by blaming current generations for what happened in the past. But that is what they say to the German governments. And very few German politicians dare to speak on this. Without Germany, the rest of Europe is embarrassed and shamefaced—they know what is going on but remain too scared to speak.

I have said this before and I will repeat it: the Palestinians have become the indirect victims of the Judeocide of the Second World War. The Jews were the direct victims, and the Palestinians are the indirect victims. They are not responsible for what happened; the responsibility rests firmly on the shoulders of Christian civilization, which wiped out six million Jews, not on the Arabs, the Muslims, or the Palestinians. I blame not just the fascist states that committed these atrocities, but also Roosevelt and Churchill, who declined to bomb the railway lines and the concentration camps where Jews were held. They knew the locations and they knew what was going on, but they refused to send bombers to destroy the railway lines and the concentration camps. Why? It wasn't a priority. The priority was to win the war; the priority was not to save the lives of Jews. Contrary to mythology, the Second World War was not fought to save the Jews.

This is the situation we confront today, which I think is going to lead to more violence, perpetuating the cycle of violence in Palestine. The tactics employed by the Israelis—the targeting of villages, the collective punishment of populations, and the assassination of individual leaders—are examples of state terror at its most naked and at its clearest.

Many Israeli dissidents, who are disgusted by what their own government is doing, are much sharper in criticizing that government than anyone in the United States. In September 2003, more than two dozen Israeli pilots signed a public statement announcing that they refused to bomb Palestinian towns and villages. It was a very sharp statement, saying, We were recruited to join the Israeli Air Force—not the Mafia; not to go out and carry out revenge killings. This created a big debate in Israel, and it is not a minor matter: No American pilot ever refused to bomb Iraq or Vietnam. Some soldiers finally stopped fighting, but no United States bomber pilot ever refused to carry out the orders of the government. These Israeli pilots who refused have a very heightened political consciousness. They were denounced and viciously attacked by politicians and the press.

This angered some decent liberal journalists in Israel. One of them, Yehuda Nuriel, published an article in a Tel Aviv weekly owned by *Maariv*, the daily tabloid newspaper, attacking the pilots and defending the Israeli government; he signed this article with a false name, A. Schicklgruber, which was Hitler's real name. No one in the newspaper knew this. Under the name of A. Schicklgruber he attacked the pilots for what they were doing, but the whole article—every single sentence—was taken from *Mein Kampf* and Hitler's speeches. This article got printed, and the editors were not troubled by its contents—until someone with a historical memory said, Oh, my God. Schicklgruber is not some old Jew in Jerusalem. It's the real name of Adolf Hitler. Nuriel was fired, naturally. But the fact that an Israeli journalist had the guts to do this is remarkable; as I often say to mainstream journalists in the United States and in Europe, Follow the example of some of your Israeli peers. They are more courageous than you.

I think this is the worst period for the Palestinians since 1948. The Israelis are now talking about killing Arafat, assuming, in line with the colonial mentality, that if you chop off the head of the leaders or imprison them, the resistance will wither—the British did this throughout the history of their empire. They even had a phrase for this absurd notion: nipping rebellion in the bud. You cut off the bud, and the flower won't grow.

But this is politics, not botany. You can nip things in the bud, or leave them to mature and then decapitate them—as the Israelis did with the Hamas leaders Ahmed Yassin and Abdel-Aziz Rantisi—but there are new generations always coming up. The children today can see clearly the conditions in which they and their families live, and the daily humiliation they face; they will mourn for Yassin and Rantisi, but tomorrow they will do the same thing. Killing off Arafat will have a similarly negligible impact; people will carry on the struggle. Any notion that it will stop is crazy—it is not going to stop at this rate. And the war against terror has become a war of terror, a war of state terror waged against people trying to fight for their freedom.

I'm troubled by your use of the term "genocide" in describing Israeli policies in Palestine.

I don't mean to imply by that that it's on the scale of what was done to the Jews of Central Europe and Germany during the Second World War. It's not genocide in that sense. It is not genocide in the sense of Rwanda. It is not even genocide in the sense of Vietnam, where two and a half million Vietnamese died in addition to the 58,000 well-memorialized Americans.

I am saying—one should be very clear on this—that the intent appears to be genocidal. When you target young children, you are basically trying to destroy the next generation. It's not genocide in the sense of numbers, because the numbers are not very large; but the intent is to punish, intimidate, and kill. I find that frightening.

Talk more about the intersection of racism in terms of framing attitudes towards not just Palestinians but Arabs and Muslims in general. Let me just read you a few comments, one from a British TV talk show host, Robert Kilroy-Silk, who wrote, "We owe the Arabs nothing. Apart from oil—which was discov-

ered, is produced, and is paid for by the West—what do they con-
tribute?" Arabs, he says, are "suicide bombers, limb-amputators,
women repressors." On this side of the Atlantic, you have people
like the bestselling author and TV pundit Ann Coulter recom-
mending that "we," that is, the West, America, "should invade
their countries, kill their leaders and convert them to Christian-
ity." You have people like Paul Weyrich and William Lind,
members of the conservative establishment, saying, "Islam is,
quite simply, a religion of war"; Billy Graham's son Franklin say-
ing that Islam is "a very evil and wicked religion," and on
and on.

The diatribes by conservatives everywhere, not just in Britain and the United States, are unending. You can find similar things in France; this French popinjay, Bernard-Henri Lévy, one of the leading official state intellectuals, wrote a book about Daniel Pearl that is filled with the most disgusting stuff about Pakistan, because he doesn't know the country, he doesn't speak the language, he doesn't know the people. But he writes a 500-page book, which is a pile of garbage. The Italian journalist Oriana Fallaci comes out with similar stuff. It's a sign of total intellectual and moral bankruptcy that this is all these people have to say. In the case of Coulter and Kilroy-Silk, it's vulgar beyond belief that they can even get away with talking like this.

Just imagine if anyone said such things about Jews. You would have the Israeli embassies going berserk denouncing them. If Coulter had made these remarks against Jews or even African Americans, in this day and age, there would have been hell to pay. But after September 11, it's open season as far as Arabs and Muslims are concerned.

The Arab regimes, or most of the Muslim governments, are utterly incapable of defending themselves or their culture against this imperial verbal onslaught. Force and awe doesn't work on ordinary people, but it certainly works on the elites who run the Arab world—because behind the force and awe are the IMF, the World Bank, and the U.S. Treasury Department. Kilroy-Silk did actually get fired from the BBC for his remarks, but his company retained the contract.

People like Coulter and Kilroy-Silk, of course, are ultraconservative, but there is another segment of people—I won't name names—who talk about Islamofascism, journalists who are liberals or former liberals but have adopted this line to justify imperial depredations in the Arab world. If the Middle East were peopled by Buddhists, you would have a massive offensive against Buddhofascism. And all these Hollywood directors who are Buddhists would not be Buddhists. They then, in that case, might have been Muslim, because it might have been a more esoteric religion.

Another voice in this cascade of abuse directed at Islam and Muslims is a high-ranking Defense Department official, Lieu-

*tenant General William Boykin, who, almost mirroring bin
Laden, says, " 'Why do they hate us?' " He answers, "Because
we're a Christian nation . . . because we are a nation of
believers. . . . Our spiritual enemy will only be defeated if we
come against them in the name of Jesus."He continues to hold his
position in the U.S. military elite.*

That is one reason I called my book *The Clash of
Fundamentalisms*—you have imperial fundamentalism,
and at the heart of that imperial fundamentalism is the
most religious country in the world. The United States, in
my opinion, is the most religious country in the world.
Many more people believe in the deity here than in large
parts of the Islamic world.

Many people in the Islamic world won't admit this in
public, so you can't do a statistical survey. But those of us
who have lived and traveled there know it to be a fact—
people are very skeptical in private, and not just intellectuals, ordinary people. You can go into the countryside
and speak to peasants, and they will make jokes about the
mullahs and religion. I remember hearing often from Pakistani peasants, "It all depends on Allah," and then, right
afterwards, "I wonder whether he'll be kind to us this
year, or will he be like he was last year."

Religion has a much stronger hold in the United
States than it does in a number of countries in the Muslim
world. Boykin, Bush, and Ashcroft are representative of
that tendency, and the Democratic leaders participate as

well—Clinton used to go to church. I don't know about
Kerry, but he will do whatever he has to do. If they tell
him, "Go and pray in a church every Sunday, that might
help you win," he will do it. If they tell him, "Go into a
synagogue to get some more votes," he will do it. He
might even go to a mosque. After all, George Bush called
in Muslim leaders.

The irony is that some of the more conservative
Muslim Americans who live in this country, many from
the South Asian diaspora, were steady Republican voters
until September 11, for an interesting assortment of reasons. First, they thought the Republicans were less harsh
on the Islamic world than the Democrats. That's been dis-
proved. But second, they genuinely felt that the Christian
right—with its attacks on abortion, homosexuality, and
promiscuity—was quite close to their own beliefs. There
was a natural affinity between conservative Muslims in
the United States and the Christian Right. But the offensive against Islam in American culture since September
11 has created a rift, which is now pushing these voters
away. I meet them from time to time in the United States,
and some of them are quite frightening. But they're learning now.

Today the big difference between Europe and the
United States is religion—Europe is not religious. The
divide on matters of politics or economics is tiny by comparison; this American piety is perplexing to Europeans,

who cannot understand the stranglehold of religion in the United States.

Talk more about Palestine and the hold it has on people's imagination. For example, why would a merchant in Multan in Pakistan, or a dockworker in Chittagong in Bangladesh, or a rice farmer in Java in Indonesia care about Palestine?

It is not necessarily because of a common religion—the cultures you cite, after all, are totally different. What they can see in Palestine under Israeli occupation is the most grotesque display of double standards. Another Arab country has been invaded, virtually dismembered, and occupied by foreign armies, supposedly because its leaders possessed weapons of mass destruction. But at the same time, they see a neighboring country that indisputably has such weapons of mass destruction, the only country in the region that might even use them—and they see this country, Israel, denying basic, elementary human rights to the Palestinian population, in Israel and in the Occupied Territories. It angers people, and it leads naturally to anger with the imperial power for acting on false premises in the case of Iraq while turning a blind eye to the obvious in Israel, since it is a long-standing ally. If the United States or the West were imposing sanctions on Israel, cutting off all subsidies to Israel, putting it under siege until it withdrew back to the 1967 borders, this anger would not exist. In fact, some of the kids attracted to terrorism would lose interest, having seen evidence that someone in the world is working to help them.

There is a movement of solidarity with Palestine, though not among states or the political classes; many young people in the United States and Europe are very angry about the situation. The name of Rachel Corrie has become immortal in Palestine.

She is the young American woman who was crushed to death by an Israeli bulldozer in Gaza.

She was deliberately crushed to death by an Israeli bulldozer. It was no accident. This was Israel's way of sending a message to Western kids who come to Palestine: We will not treat you any differently. You come and stand by the Palestinians, and you will be crushed. Rachel Corrie was not the only victim; Tom Hurndall, a young Briton, was shot in Gaza and died after a long time in a coma. This is how they operate—they murder the kids who come from the West to stand side by side with the Palestinians to prevent their houses from being demolished.

They have turned the Israeli embassies into total propaganda machines for the Zionist state, touting a new, big wave of anti-Semitism sweeping the world, which is nonsense. Anti-Semitism exists in certain parts of the world—genuine anti-Semitism—but they confuse this deliberately with hostility to Israel. If you are critical of what Israel is doing to the Palestinians—the punishments it's inflicting, the kids it's killing, the lands it's occupying—if you're hostile to the settlers in Palestinian land, you are an anti-Semite. And if you are a Jew, then you are a self-hating Jew. Israeli embassies all over Europe are devoted to this propaganda effort—they are concerned because the Europeans are skeptical about Israeli actions in the territories. In the United States, they don't need to worry, because the House and the Senate essentially passed a blank check of support to Israel. It's unheard of—they don't give that sort of support to their own government, but they're prepared to give that support to Israel. There is an Israeli offensive against dissent, abroad and at home.

What would you say to the argument that's made that Israel has been very convenient for the various Arab emirs and sheikhs and tyrants as a kind of diversion from their own shortcomings and oppressive behavior?

This is true, but increasingly the populations of these countries have begun to see through their leaders. The Saudi monarchy is not popular in Saudi Arabia. The Egyptian regime is not popular in its own country, which is why it doesn't permit open, free elections—because they know they would be defeated. These sheikhs who rule the Gulf states, these little imperial petrol stations, are equally unpopular. Can you imagine a small-town petrol station in California or Texas guarded by hundreds and thousands of foreign soldiers? That is the situation in the Gulf. The largest American military base outside the United States is in the tiny principality of Qatar, which has a population that is less than Los Angeles. But they have the largest base, the Al Udeid base, from which the most advanced planes can take off and land—where the planes that bombed Baghdad took off.

This is why all this talk about taking democracy to the Arab world is such a pile of crap, if you will pardon the expression, because the only regimes the Americans like working with are those that can guarantee the flow of oil at affordable rates. The Saudis do it, the Gulf sheikhs do it. Saddam cooperated for some time, and he fell out with the Americans and refused to play along; the Iranians don't do it any longer either. This is the fight that has been going on—in my books I refer to the wars in that region as oil wars. These are the wars for oil, which have been fought on Muslim terrain by imperial powers—the British and the United States. Israel occupies a very important place in this arrangement. You're right that the Saudis and other regimes have used the existence of Israel to distract their citizens with blustering rhetoric, to appear to oppose American plans—but when it comes to concrete measures, they do absolutely nothing.

Mudhaffar al-Nawab wrote a poem some years ago on an Arab summit, a very satirical and vicious poem called "Summits." Many people are embarrassed by this poem because it's so vicious, and some say it's a bit crude, but I don't think so. It displays anger. He sort of describes the Arab leaders who gather at these summits as sheep, rams, and goats. In one place he says that suddenly a goat walks into the conference chamber, and the goat urinates. They all inspect the piss. Ah, the goat has pissed. How interesting it is. Let us look at it more closely. Let us inspect it. And the poem goes on and on like this. I was thinking of Mudhaffar's poem when this latest summit which was meant to take place was canceled because the leaders could not even agree whether to have a summit or not. This is the state of the leadership of the Arab world. Obviously, the West has always interfered and intervened, but here one has to say that the Arab leaders, who had the opportunities to change the situation and transform it forever, failed, in part because they were quarreling with each other. In the late 1950s and 1960s, there was a real chance to create a genuine United Arab Republic with three concurrent capitals—Cairo, Damascus, and Baghdad—and it did not happen. We now pay the price.

Talk about how elements of the Palestinian national movement have themselves internalized the sense of being colonized. In particular, their consistent appeals to the principal patron of their adversary to somehow liberate them, to do right by them.

Edward Said described Oslo as a Palestinian Versailles, where, in return for a few crumbs, they basically agreed to surrender. The Palestinian leadership thought they might get a tiny state out of this, a state that would at least be functional—but they didn't even get that. Instead, all that the Israelis were prepared to offer them was tiny Bantustans. Instead of using the Oslo period to mobilize their population and the rest of world public opinion by saying, "This is what we expected, and we're not getting it," Arafat and his entourage were busy making money, recycling the money being donated for lots of decent projects in Palestine. They started eating up this money, looting their own country.

The second intifada was not just an uprising against the Zionist occupation of Palestine; it was also a protest against the corruption of the Palestinian leadership. I think the Palestinians themselves might have deposed Arafat had it not been for Sharon's new offensive against him. When the Israelis cut off his electricity, they made him into a hero again, just by attacking him. Those images of Arafat, photographed in the candlelight, made him look like a Rembrandt painting; after this attack on Arafat, people gave him a break.

The question you pose is an important one. We have paid a terrible price for the decision of the secular Palestinian leadership to cave in to the United States. It means that the radical opposition is in the hands of the religious group Hamas, whom I defend despite disagreeing with many of their tactics because they are the only people defending the Palestinians against daily brutalities. But, to be honest, it's not in the interests of the Palestinian people to be led by a group which is so deeply religious, because—leaving aside all the other reasons—Palestine is not simply composed of Muslims. There are many Christian Palestinians as well, and we don't want to drive them out; they've been very active in the struggle.

But the PLO made the fateful mistake of agreeing to Oslo, and then participating in the farce that took place at Camp David. When I look at the pictures from that summit, the paternal familiarity with which Clinton and Barak treated Arafat reminds me of the way feudal lords used to treat their favorite servants—that's the way they were treating Arafat. They even tried to restrain him physically to prevent his leaving Camp David after he realized that he was being offered no more than the status quo. The Palestinian leaders saw this happening, but they were not capable of devising any alternatives.

When the Israelis agreed to negotiate at Oslo, they insisted it be with the PLO—then in exile in Tunis—and not with the local leadership of the first intifada. The local leadership, which essentially forced the Israelis to Oslo to try and negotiate a settlement, were honest and incorruptible. Even the PLO leaders in the West Bank were very different from those in exile. There was a deliberate decision to negotiate with the PLO in exile and to force the internal leaders, PLO and non-PLO, of the first intifada, to accept Arafat's sovereignty. When you see Arafat's spokesmen on television today, on CNN or whatever, their body language is pathetic, trying to please the imperial masters: Look how reasonable we are. Look how we crawl on our knees in front of you. We are on our knees, and the Israelis still come and kick us down—that's what they've been reduced to.

Palestine desperately needs national leadership which is going to pursue the struggle for this century. I hope by the end of this century we will see a Palestinian state that is meaningful—a proper state with contiguous borders and at least half of the old state of greater Israel—or, if that does not happen, that Palestinians win the struggle to become equal citizens in a unified state of Palestine-Israel. The Zionist establishment is against both, and that is their great weakness—they can't prevent both forever.

When Sharon came to Washington in April 2004, the United States essentially signed off on the annexation of large swaths of the West Bank and its very precious aquifer. Let's not forget the water resources that are involved. Curiously, there was no mention of the annexed Golan Heights of Syria—that's completely disappeared from any kind of public scrutiny—or East Jerusalem, for that matter, which was annexed by Israel in violation of international law.

We have to be very careful when we talk about international law. You are, of course, absolutely right—there are UN resolutions denouncing all this. But international law only functions when the largest, most powerful state in the world wants it to do so. It cannot function unless that state accepts it. The United States has always been cavalier in the enforcement of international law—in the wars they've fought, with the people they've killed, in what they continue to do in Iraq. So I'm afraid it's not international law that is going to come to help the Palestinians. What they will have to do at some point is make that part of the world ungovernable unless they get their rights.

There has historically been a notion of a united front. What if there were a real coalition of nations and peoples coming together to resist the empire? Could that not have an effect?

Absolutely, but only if at least one bloc emerged that was hostile to the American empire, whether in the Far East or elsewhere, which could provide some support, and some cover to the beleaguered populations of Palestine and Iraq. If the Latin American states and the Asian and South Asian states began to say, "We don't care what the United States says or does, we're going to help the Palestinians; we're going to send volunteers; we're going to help them with arms; we're going to help the struggle"—that would also make a great difference. Why would they do that? Because this is the last remaining colonial struggle of the twentieth century. Obviously, if that were to happen, it would change the situation in the Middle East.

But even the wretched Arab governments that surround the Palestinians don't support the struggle, which creates a very bad impression for the rest of the world. If the Arab League had some muscle and made these appeals to the rest of the world, it would help, but they do not. I sometimes get very depressed when I consider this situation, and then I think the only way forward is for a wave of democratic revolutions—democratic in the sense that they reflect the will of the people in that region—to sweep aside the corrupt imperial satrapies that dominate the Middle East. That would transform the situation overnight. Washington would then face an interesting problem—they would have to make a choice between establishing relations with these new regimes and continuing to back Israel—quite a test for the imperial leadership. The joke in Left circles in the United States is that if the Americans were to dump Israel for its own imperial reasons, to put pressure on them and move them out, the only two people in the country to stand up to save Israel would be Noam Chomsky and Norman Finkelstein.

Expand further on the reluctance, particularly among liberals in the United States, to talk about Palestine in concrete

*terms. Let me read you something that Edward Said wrote about
his dear friend, Eqbal Ahmad, the Pakistani scholar-activist.
Ahmad was very active on Palestine. But Said asks, "How many
friends avoid the subject? How many colleagues want nothing of
Palestine's controversy? How many* bien pensant *liberals have
time for Bosnia and Somalia and South Africa and Nicaragua
and human and civil rights everywhere on Earth, but not for
Palestine and Palestinians?"*

Edward is absolutely right on—it is very noticeable.
It was noticeable from 1967 onwards. Prior to that, not
too many people thought of Palestine. But since 1967,
this has been a real weakness among liberals. Not the
Left, I would say, which in Europe certainly has taken up
the cause of the Palestinians. Many, many people on the
far Left have defended the Palestinians, and still do, including many people of Jewish origin.

My own education on this subject did not come in Pakistan. When I was growing up, Palestine was barely mentioned, because Pakistan was then part of the network of
American security pacts—first the Baghdad pact, then,
after Iraq fell in 1958, it became SEATO, the Southeast
Asia Treaty Organization. Palestine was barely talked
about in that world; we were very ignorant about it. I first
learned about the real atrocities that had been carried out
in Palestine by the Zionists from radicals of Jewish origin:
Maxime Rodinson, Ernest Mandel, Akiva Orr, Moshé
Machover, Nathan Weinstock, Isaac Deutscher, Michael

Löwy, and others. These people basically provided my generation, in the 1960s, with an education on this topic. They were very hard-line, hard-core anti-Zionists. Now there are many more of them, and they are now even more hostile to Israel—so there is a small minority of people who defend the Palestinians today.

But this is a time when the Palestinian struggle should be *the* central cause in world politics, alongside Iraq. For many people, of course, it is. The dual occupation of the Arab East is increasingly being taken up as a rallying cry. But many liberals in Europe and in the United States who are very hostile to the occupation of Iraq will not mention Palestine at all. As I mentioned earlier, this is largely the result of guilt for what was done to the Jews by the Third Reich. For others, it's purely cynical—Israel is a close ally of the United States, and we'd better not offend the United States. In the United States itself, the stranglehold of pro-Israeli sentiment is so strong that I think there has only been one op-ed piece in the *New York Times,* by Noam Chomsky, denouncing the wall. Otherwise, no one gives a damn.

It's not simply due to the might of the Zionist lobby, though that is very strong. I don't think that's the only reason, however: In the United States, they feel that Israel is the oasis of Western interests—it's a country like us. In some ways that's true, because the original emigrants came from Europe, and many of the settlers are actually from the United States of America. When they appear on

American television, people can identify with them, because many of them speak with American accents.

There are other people who refuse to denounce Israel because that would mean denouncing the United States—indeed, you can hardly denounce Israel without denouncing the United States, and the policies of Clinton and Bush alike. The population of the United States, as with many other issues, is blissfully unaware of the realities on the ground; the bulk of the political, cultural, and media elite is staunchly pro-Israel, as we can see so clearly in the election campaign under way at the moment. On the question of Israel, John Kerry, the Democratic presidential contender, says he is 100 percent in agreement with George W. Bush. He went even further than Bush by defending, where Bush had been a little less strident, the killing of the Hamas leaders. Kerry released a statement describing how proud he had been to visit Israel, and his joy at riding in an Israeli jet bomber, which he had flown for a bit to see for himself what the ground looked like underneath. The Palestinians—and the basic human rights violations that take place every day—didn't rate a mention. When the world's largest and most powerful state is run by such politicians, why should the Palestinian leadership pin its hopes on them? In time, a leadership will emerge that will break from the United States, and when that begins to happen, the struggle will commence in earnest, and we will see portions of American public opinion shift as well.

There does exist a formation called the Palestine National Initiative. Mustafa Barghouti is active in it. Edward Said was one of its founders. The PNI is a democratic, secular movement. But I am interested in discussing the fact that even people with our views use the terms of propaganda—for example, calling these colonies "settlements" and calling colonizers "settlers," which has a very benign resonance, particularly in the United States. We're in the American West right now—it was settled by brave pioneers who came and conquered the savage Indians.

We are all partially guilty of that, it's true. When I use the word "settler," however, the image I have is not of the United States, because I don't live here, but of the French settlers in Algeria or the Dutch settlers in South Africa, who were defeated. Many of us in Europe use that word in the hope that they will suffer the same fate as the Boers—after hundreds of years in South Africa—and the French in Algeria.

The big difference between the Israelis and the other colonial enterprises is that the French in Algeria, and even the Dutch in South Africa, if they had been pushed or driven out, had places to go back to. The French went back to France; if the Dutch had been driven out, they would have gone back to Holland, and probably then been used to police Indonesia. In any event, they had a place, but for many Israeli Jews, there is no such thing anymore. These Brooklyn guys who go and impose themselves on the Palestinian lands can always come back to

Brooklyn, of course. But for large numbers of Israelis, there is nowhere to return. The Palestinian leaders have accepted this, as has the Arab world. No one talks now about driving the Israelis into the sea, as they used to in some of the belligerent rhetoric of the 1950s, which the Zionists invoke constantly—"We are a small, beleaguered little country. They want to drive us into the sea." No one says that anymore—no one serious, that is—because people have accepted that these guys are going to be with us. All that is at stake is a way of living together. They can't even accept that—they don't seem to accept it, at least. They're still posing as the offended party; that's what is disgusting. If the Israeli leaders stood up and apologized for what they did, just one public apology— "We are sorry for what we did"—it would make a world of difference. But they will not make that apology.

This revisionist Israeli historian, Benny Morris, who is without any doubt a serious historian, did an interview with *Ha'aretz,* which we translated and published in the *New Left Review,* just to show the thinking of these people. Morris essentially said, Yes, there were ethnic cleansings; yes, we expelled nearly a million people; yes, there were rapes. But so what? Others deny that this happened. But Morris can't deny it, because he has seen the papers— and he doesn't want to deny it. He defends it as necessary to build the Israeli state and goes on to say the pity is that they didn't kick out all the Palestinians when they had the chance. He compares Israel's actions to what the early

Protestant fundamentalist settlers in the Americas did to
the Native Americans—compares them with no shame at
all. A superior civilization; a colonial project. Benny
Morris's parents are English Jews, so presumably the
legacy of the British Empire had some effect on him. This
is one of Israel's most prominent and senior historians.
He's been denounced by left-wing Israeli historians, and
even the Zionist establishment is embarrassed by his
statements. But at least he has said it; he's laid it all down
on paper. It's very significant that he's done this, compar-
ing the fate of the Palestinians to that of the Native Americans. People like myself used to invoke this comparison,
and the Israelis protested that this was slander: "What an
outrageous comparison; we've been so kind to the Palestinians, but they won't listen to us—they're the ones who
fight us, who bomb us. What have we ever done to
them—all we wanted to do was live in peace." That argument no longer holds any water.

*How would you respond to the traditional Zionist argument
that there is only one state for the Jewish people while there are
more than twenty Arab states? Why don't those Arab states absorb
the Palestinian population and integrate them into their societies? Only Jordan has offered citizenship to the Palestinians.*

The question is this: Why should the Palestinians be
forced to settle anywhere else? Why shouldn't they have
the right, like other people in the world, to live in their

villages, to live in their lands? They don't want to move out of their homes—they were forced out. They're quite happy to be citizens with equal rights in an Israeli state, provided they are not permanently mistreated, mal-treated, punished, locked up, or humiliated. What is wrong with that? Coexistence has played a very strong part in the liberal cultural tradition of Judaism—it's the combination of Zionism and some Jewish fundamental-ists that has created this monstrosity.

None of the Arab states were ever purely Muslim states. They had Christian populations, and there were Jewish populations in Cairo and Baghdad—very large Jewish populations. What happened to them? Nothing, until Israel was formed and the Israelis sent in people to drive those Jews out—they bombed cafés in Baghdad to frighten the Jews there into emigrating to Israel. I think a state created on this basis, quite honestly—leaving aside the fact that it's wrong or immoral—it's not even in the interests of the majority of Jews to live in a ghetto state. All your life you've been put in ghettos; you've been try-ing to get out of these ghettos, trying to integrate. Now you want to build a ghetto state in a part of the world which isn't yours.

I think we have to argue, on principle, for the right of all states to be multicultural. The only reason to create an ethnic, racist state in that part of the world is to drive out the remaining Palestinians; the wall that is being built is partially designed to do that. But it will not work. Sooner or later even the majority of the Jews of Israel will rebel against this life, because it's not a very nice life for them.

You've written about and studied extensively the history of Al Andalus, the syncretic civilization that existed in the Iberian Peninsula, where there was a highly developed multicultural society. Those people were driven out. If they were not forcibly converted to Christianity, they were expelled or killed. And most of the Jews then wound up where?

History is full of ironies. When I was researching material for my novel *Shadows of the Pomegranate Tree,* which is set in the fifteenth century on the Iberian Peninsula, I found amazing things. One of the nicest things was the coexistence of the three *religions*—Christianity, Islam, Judaism—which had good effects on all of them. Until Catholic fundamentalism became determined to end that experiment and create a new European identity, one free of Jews and Muslims, since both were regarded as outsiders and "the Other." Throughout the period of Muslim Spain, or Al Andalus, there were barely any reported cases of pogroms against the Jews. They lived in comfort, they had high positions, they worked with the Muslims or under the Muslim rulers, worked with them, and were central to the existence of Al Andalus. Everyone knows this.

The historian Benzion Netanyahu—the father of the former Israeli prime minister—has constantly tried to find little episodes in medieval Spain where some Jew was persecuted. I could find episodes where Muslims were persecuted—so what? The point is, it was a different period, in which Jews and Muslims grew up together and lived together. When they were expelled, lots of Jews went to Morocco, many more went to Istanbul and the Ottoman Empire, and the Ottoman Empire then sent them as administrators, people working for the great Ottoman state, back into the Arab world. Many of the communities of Damascus were built or grew during the Ottoman period. That's the tragedy and irony of all this.

Let me add another irony, not strictly related to the Jewish question. I was in Spain some weeks ago for the launch of the Spanish edition of *Bush in Babylon*. At the same time, the new Spanish leadership, which had decided to withdraw Spanish troops from Iraq, was being inaugurated. It was a very joyous atmosphere, a victory for the antiwar movement in Europe and a big defeat for Bush and Blair in Spain. But you know what amazed me? I saw a map of Iraq in *El País,* and the Spanish conservative government, the successors of Franco, had named the Spanish occupation base in Iraq "Al Andalus." I was so angered by this that I denounced it at my press conferences—I said, "How dare you despoil and use the name of a great cultural, human experiment which lasted four or five hundred years in your part of the world? It's either ignorance or the height of cynicism. If Aznar had been more honest and wanted to reflect real history, that base should have been called 'Ferdinand and Isabella Base' or 'Archbishop Cisneros Base,' but not 'Al Andalus.' "

Richard Cohen is a nationally syndicated columnist in the United States. Recently he had a piece where he notes that the United Nations is quick to pass resolutions condemning Israel for human rights violations in Palestine but that there are very few such resolutions about human rights violations going on in Egypt or Saudi Arabia or any of the Arab states. This is a typical argument. Respond to it.

Who has created the regimes in these states? I would be very happy to see the end of the Saudi monarchy. I would love to see a democratic election in Saudi Arabia. Who stops it from happening? It's not the United Nations, weak though it is—it is the United States of America. What power does the United Nations have in Saudi Arabia? The only time the American establishment has wobbled in relation to Saudi Arabia was following September 11, because they were embarrassed by the fact that the bulk of the bombers were Saudi citizens from the Hijaz. They were not poor Afghan peasants; most were Saudis and one was Egyptian—two of the closest Arab allies of the United States. Who is stopping democracy there? It's not Islam that is preventing it—the Islamists in both these countries would love to have an election, because they have a fair chance of winning.

This is what our old friend Sam Huntington has now begun to call the democratic paradox. What is the demo-

cratic paradox? The democratic paradox, for Mr. Huntington, is that if you allow democracy to emerge in these
countries, they might elect governments that we don't
like. But surely that is the whole point of democracy—
that the people have the right to elect who they want. This
is why the United States has never encouraged democracy in the Middle East. Columnists like Cohen and nu-
merous others—it's like a plague of locusts in the
American media—write this nonsense, but they don't
know what their own government has been doing in that
region for the last half century. This whole system has
been created to facilitate imperial interests. Who else
would have created it? Did the people of Kuwait want to
be ruled by their sheikh?

*In Palestine, there is a great asymmetry of force and military
might—you have a clear preponderance on one side and very little on the other. It mirrors, to some degree, the situation in India
at the time Gandhi launched his nonviolent resistance
movement—against a colonial power with liberal pretensions
about the rule of law. Israel, like the British, embraces liberal
rhetoric about law and human rights—could the Palestinian
trump card in this situation be nonviolent resistance? Eqbal
Ahmad, for one, proposed that the refugees in the surrounding
Arab countries march on the borders of Israel and say, "We want to
go home."*

It would be an event that would dominate the news
for no more than four days. It's a nice idea, but one has to

take into account that the Zionist leadership is not the British Empire in India. The British Empire in India could only maintain its rule with the support of large sectors of the local elite—the empire only functioned because the feudal lords in India, the princes who controlled both the land and the peasants, cooperated. But when the national movement emerged and began to affect the peasants—Gandhi's greatest appeal was to the Indian peasantry—then the empire became untenable.

The situation in Israel is totally different. This is a state with nuclear weapons, with the fifth-largest army in the world, a very effective and brutal fighting force. It is conceivable that they would permit demonstrations—they probably would—but if these coalesced into a large nonviolent resistance movement, they would crush it. They would crush it brutally.

But don't you think, for example, that suicide bombers play right into the hands of the Israelis?

They do and they don't. It's not a tactic I particularly favor, but consider what some senior Zionist leaders have been saying: let's look again at Avraham Burg, the former speaker of the Knesset and former head of the Jewish Agency, who wrote that

Israel, having ceased to care about the children of the Palestinians, should not be surprised when they come washed in hatred and blow themselves up in

the centers of Israeli escapism. They consign themselves to Allah in our places of recreation, because
their own lives are torture. They spill their own
blood in our restaurants in order to ruin our ap-
petites, because they have children and parents at
home who are hungry and humiliated.

He said this because he realizes that you cannot disso-
ciate the suicide bombings from the reality of the
occupation—all the reporting, however, separates the
two. You must understand the realities of the occupation
of Palestine, the daily realities—forcing people to stand
for hours at checkpoints while you search them and hu-
miliate them; refusing to allow pregnant women to be
taken to the hospital, which has caused miscarriages—all
of these things breed desperation. So the Palestinians
have resorted to suicide bombings; I don't like these tactics, but they are linked to the reality of the occupation.

*Do you think that Israel was a factor in the U.S. attack on
Iraq?*

It was a factor, but I don't accept that it was the dominant factor or that the Israelis organized the war, or anything like that. The Israelis wanted to end the regime in
Iraq because they saw it as the only regime with the potential to take them on, if it so wished; they have never
liked the Iraqi regime, precisely because it was an independent Arab state. During the Iran-Iraq War, even as the

United States and Britain were backing Iraq, the Israelis were actually giving spare parts for Chieftain tanks to the Iranians. Menachem Begin was asked, "What is your position on the Iraq war?" And he said, "When goyim fights goyim, all I can do is sit back and applaud." But they were very nervous about Iraq—don't forget that they bombed Iraq's nuclear reactor in 1981, with U.S. permission. There is no doubt at all that the Israelis wanted the invasion of Iraq. What the Israeli ambassador to Washington said was, Don't stop now—go and finish the job with Syria and Iran. There is no doubt about where they stand.

There is also no doubt that senior Israeli officials met with Ahmed Chalabi before the invasion of Iraq, and Chalabi promised them that Iraq would recognize Israel within a few months of his taking charge. Today, Chalabi himself isn't recognized by anyone, so he's in no position to deliver for the Israelis, but his promises certainly made them happy, and they obviously backed the invasion.

The American occupation of Iraq could have followed the old, time-honored British formula: find a layer of the local elite, real natives, and make a deal to secure their support and cooperation. For that, of course, you need time, which the British had in their day. But the Americans could have adapted this scheme—by leaving the Iraqi army intact, perhaps, and making use of it. This might not have worked, but the Americans didn't even try it—they opted for the Israeli methods of colonization: Hit hard; punish towns, villages, and families. Destroy the villages of resistance fighters or the homes of their families.

Where did Israelis learn this? They learned it from their German oppressors; this is what the Germans used to do in the Second World War: punish whole towns at once. Power that is based on brutality, force, and occupation always remains precarious, unstable.

Collective punishment?

The Germans imposed collective punishment. The United States took it to new heights during the Vietnam War. The Israelis did it to the Palestinians. And now the Americans are doing it to the Iraqis—they chose the Israeli model but are less precise and less intelligent. That is how they want to run Iraq: keep their own bases there, stay in those bases to reduce U.S. casualties, and go out in big numbers with air cover to hit the Iraqis when they have to. It's not going to work.

Have you thought about the interesting symmetry between what happened in Palestine in 1948 and what took place just a few months earlier on the Indian subcontinent? Again, the legacies of imperialism—cartographers come along, draw maps; peoples are separated; wars ensue. These are two gaping wounds. If someone were to look at planet Earth from outer space, they would see the blood leaching from Palestine and from Kashmir.

There are similarities. As I have said, it is always the case that when empires rule, they do so in their own interests. And the way they rule is by dividing populations, separating ethnic communities, using any leverage they can obtain to make sure that the country runs properly. And the country can only run properly when they use one section of the community against another. They did it in India very successfully. But the end result was something which no one had foreseen—the partition of that subcontinent.

Let's talk about the role of culture in resistance. We have discussed poetry in previous interviews. You mentioned Abdelrahman Munif, the great novelist who died in January of 2004. In fact, you wrote a piece about him in The Nation, *virtually the only mention of the passing of one of the most significant writers in the Arab world in this era.*

Munif, I think, was one of the most gifted novelists and artists produced in the Arab world, together with Naguib Mahfouz, with whom he's been compared, although they were very different, both in style and in their political temperaments. Mahfouz is also a great novelist, no question about that, but what gave Munif the edge, in my opinion, was that he was born of a Saudi father and an Iraqi mother, and knew the Saudi regions extremely well. His set of novels, *Cities of Salt,* provided us with a picture of Saudi Arabia that has not been equaled. It's a set of five novels, three of which have been translated into English, though they are not published in paperback in most parts of the world.

The novel played a role in the Arab world similar to the one it used to play in nineteenth-century Europe; it became a means of intervention. A new novel by Munif, by Mahfouz—or, as in Latin America, by Garcia Marquez—could be bought at kiosks in the streets, and people read them avidly. This interplay between politics and culture has always been very strong in the Arab world. Even in a world dominated now by rubbishy television which repeats American series and tries to produce local versions of Western reality programs, this old tradition persists; for the common people it still exists, and these novels are still read and discussed.

There is a lot of cultural ferment in the United States, in terms of resistance. There are musicians like Michael Franti, a prominent hip-hop artist, who has composed and sung many trenchant critiques of U.S. power. There are singers and performers like David Rovics, Saul Williams, and Sarah Jones. Tim Robbins has a play in New York at the Public Theater called Embedded. *Are there similar things going on in Britain, where you live? You were planning on writing an opera on Ayatollah Khomeini.*

That's one of my projects on the back burner. It is my idea to do a serious opera—partially serious, at least, and partially comic. But for that you need Phillip Glass to do the music and probably a great director to produce it. I wrote a play last year called *The Illustrious Corpse,* which ran in central London and in Leicester—a big, ferocious satirical attack on Blair and all his works. A cabinet minister is found dead, a home secretary, a black politician. His wife admits that she has killed him, but she says she killed him because she knew he was going to do bad things in the world—she's carried out a preemptive strike. She wants to tell people why she did it, because of every single principle he betrayed. And she thinks a jury will acquit her. The state then tries to stop the trial from happening, and the spin doctors inform the media that he died of a heart attack.

Lots of kids and young people came to see the play, which was great. A British band called Asian Dub Foundation has put one of my speeches to music and, if memory serves me right, one of Noam Chomsky's, too, which I'm dying to hear. The kids tell me, "We heard your speech. Did you listen to the music under it?" There are lots of enterprising young people, in the best sense of the word, who are resisting, and this is sort of universal. Some of the hip-hop resistance in the United States travels far and wide, like everything else from the United States—one should never forget that. It has a positive impact.

A dramatic new development has been the growth of independent Arab satellite networks, like Al-Jazeera, Al-Arabiya, and others.

Certainly Al-Jazeera has been a major development in the Arab world. They do what the BBC says it does: they really are objective. They put out footage, they air arguments, they interview people from both sides. That is seen as a threat, because the mainstream media is so carefully managed—crudely in the United States and cleverly in Britain, but managed nonetheless. Every single television news program in Britain or the United States, if you watch them one after another, leads with the same stories. How could that happen if the news were not managed, if they were not told these are the key stories of the day? Exactly the same footage is used. Al-Jazeera, and to a certain extent Al-Arabiya, break that mold. They make their own news and make their own headlines, and they challenge the monopoly of the media moguls who own and control the Western media.

This challenge is seen as a real threat—Al-Jazeera television headquarters was attacked in Afghanistan, Al-Jazeera journalists were killed in Baghdad, Al-Jazeera journalists covering the uprising in Falluja were targeted. No one was killed, mercifully, but they were targeted. The only journalism that the West likes is embedded journalism: "Come with us and you will be safe. If you don't come with us, you might die. You certainly will if you're an Arab. And even if you're a Westerner, be careful." I'm really happy that nothing has happened to Bob Fisk in Iraq—I worry about him sometimes, because he goes into the field a lot and sends back these amazing reports.

The emergence of Al-Jazeera has transformed journalism in the Arab world, because no one watches state television anymore; everyone, whether you're in Cairo or Damascus, watches Al-Jazeera. You get it on a satellite dish. Even here in the United States many people watch Al-Jazeera. During the run-up to the Iraq war, I think two million Europeans subscribed, including many who couldn't speak Arabic, just so they could see the different images. This is a very positive development.

How long it will last remains to be seen, because Al-Jazeera shares one thing with the United States: they're both based in Qatar. The largest U.S. base, the Al Udeid base, is in Qatar, and not too far from it is the headquarters of Al-Jazeera. This makes some people nervous—how long will this last? Will the Americans find ways of curbing Al-Jazeera?

We have also seen the emergence in the United States of shows like *Democracy Now,* and your own shows, which are broadcast everywhere. People in Britain who listen to a station called Resonance FM, which I didn't even know existed, have called me to say, "We heard you being interviewed by David Barsamian." I said, "Where? Have you been in the States?" They said, "No, in London." These things circulate widely because people are desperate for alternative means of information. Free Speech TV is expanding, *CounterSpin* in Canada is seen in different parts of the world. The monopoly that the establishment controlled from the 1960s until the 1990s is starting to show some cracks, although it has not been broken; the alternative media in the West has not yet produced anything that can rival the monopoly, but there is now the possibility of accessing voices that can't be heard in the mainstream media.

We're in the month of April, which T. S. Eliot called "the cruelest month." Certainly it's been the month with the highest number of American deaths and casualties in Iraq, and also the highest number of Iraqis wounded and killed. We don't know the exact numbers, because we're not told by the Pentagon—they appear not to be interested. At a recent press conference in Baghdad, one of the Arab journalists asked about the images from inside Falluja being broadcast on Al-Jazeera, showing Iraqi civilians who had been killed by the American forces laying siege to that city. The American general, Mark Kimmitt, simply dismissed the Arab journalist's question. If you don't like what you're seeing, Kimmitt replied, "change the channel."

That is twenty-first century America in a nutshell. Here in the United States, if you don't like what you're seeing, you can change the channel, but you still get the same thing—like the Bruce Springsteen song, "57 Channels (And Nothin' On)." At least in the Arab world, you have an alternative.

For Kimmitt, a Pentagon spokesman, to dismiss the killing of Iraqi civilians like that displays a brutality and a contempt for the people whose country you're occupying, who you claim you went to save—but this is hardly surprising. What should be surprising—or maddening—is that the images of what American troops did to punish the people of Falluja were not seen on American and European television. The Ministry of Defense in Britain, like the Pentagon, strictly regulates access to war zones to make sure images like these never reach the televisions back home. This control of the media is very much a part of the war effort. The media has become a central player in the war, because the authorities depend on it to convince the people.

A final issue worth noting: People get very upset in the West when foreign businessmen or mercenaries are targeted in Iraq. They shouldn't be angry. The Iraqis are merely saying, This is our country, and we don't want your corporations in here. And this has been very effective; lots of Western firms are withdrawing their people from Iraq. Yesterday I was speaking at the *Los Angeles Times* book fair, and Nicholas von Hoffman, a senior journalist, said, Look, we were shown those hanged bodies in Falluja, but at least those men had been killed before they were lynched. Don't forget the images we have seen in this country—of burnt and charred African American bodies hanging from trees while people picnic underneath. Don't forget that. That is this country.

AFTERWORD

Four More Years:
Peace? War? Each Year Worse
than the Year Before?

The United States is one of the most striking examples of the fact that the spread of modern science and technology—the only genuinely universal aspect of European capitalist civilization—need not be accompanied by the spread of secularism. In a country where 60 percent of the population believes in Satan and 89 percent in the deity, Bush's electoral triumph has highlighted the principal differences between Western Europe and the United States: not politics and economics, but war and religion. Both came together in November 2004 as the evangelist wing of the U.S. Marines prepared to assault Fallujah. Reports from the front described how a group of the assembled troops swayed to Christian rock, praised Old Testament heroes (it was dear young David, of course, against the Philistine terrorists), denounced the

Iraqi resistance as "Satan's creatures," and pleaded with Jesus to help them.

Their chaplain, a robust preacher named Horne, told the worshippers they were there to bring the Iraqis "freedom from oppression, rape, torture and murder. . . . We ask you God to bless us in that effort." As the marines lined up, Horne sprinkled them with holy oil to protect them—which, given the circumstances, was appropriate. Perhaps it was some other God who pushed them in the opposite direction: to oppress, torture, rape, and murder prisoners and shoot wounded freedom fighters in the head.

God was much in evidence back home as well. His earthly creatures—helped by experienced Satanists like Karl Rove—had fulminated against the sodomites and the fetus-killers and their friend Kerry and helped to elect George W. Bush. The incumbent obtained three million more votes than his Democratic opponent. In 2000, Gore won the popular vote. This time, despite some jiggery-pokery, the victory was convincing and the Supreme Court was not required to green-light a flawed election. Those who insisted the election had been rigged were wasting their time. The overall percentage may have been narrow, but there could be no doubt as to the victory. It was foolish and self-defeating to pretend otherwise.

If John Kerry had developed a clear antiwar stance and gone on the offensive, he might still have lost but

U.S. citizens would have benefited from the education, and as the situation in Iraq deteriorated further, it would have been easier to isolate Bush and his cohorts in the U.S. Congress. On its own the war damaged Bush's credibility, but not enough. The brutal fact is that the U.S. casualty rate in Iraq was simply not high enough to disgust the population sufficiently and turn it away from war. So a president who, together with his team, lied consistently and shamelessly to drag his country into war has been elected. If the war goes seriously wrong, as it shows every sign of doing over the next year, the Republicans will only pay a price if there is an opposition. Senators like the defeated Democrat Tom Daschle, a man who gives opportunism a bad name, are no help at all. Desperate Daschle's advertising campaign showed him hugging Bush, an image designed to promote war, not gay marriage. In this case the South Dakotans got the message and voted for the real thing.

When an electorate wishes to defeat an incumbent it does so regardless of the opposition. Earlier this year in India, the electorate defeated the far-right government and elected an opposition headed by an Italian woman.

In the past here too, Hubert Humphrey, defending the Democratic Party's war in Vietnam, lost to Nixon, who was compelled to end the war and whose chicanery in delaying the decision helped to unlock the Watergate. Prior to that, Harry Truman, the architect of the Korean War, chose not to run for reelection, and the Democratic candidate, Adlai Stevenson, lost to Eisenhower, who did agree to a cease-fire and brought most of the boys back home. This time Bush used Osama bin Laden and socio-cultural issues to mobilize the most reactionary sections of the electorate on the basis of lowest-common-denominator politics. A majority of the electorate went along with him.

Bush's real victory lies in the panic exhibited by the Democrats before and after the election. Kerry was a weak and pathetic choice. Flaunting his war record in Vietnam and parading his credentials as a hunter did little to enhance his character. After their defeat, the Demo-crats rushed to cross the line and crowd the enemy's field. In appointing Senator Harry Reid from Nevada—an uninspiring, teetotaling, abortion-hating Mormon—as the new Senate minority leader, they appear to have given up on politics. They should be careful. If Reid helps them to do better in the next congressional elections, Karl Rove will launch an anti-bigamy campaign. Reposition-ing themselves by adopting the opposition's social agenda is counterproductive and might even push left-liberals in the direction of a Third Party. If the Democrats decide not to oppose the privatization of social security or what the Republicans have done in California—truly vicious and heartbreaking cuts in hospitals and education at all levels that have massively harmed the poor and harm them more every day—they will become even more ir-relevant as an opposition than they were in 2004.

The hard-right social agenda espoused by Cheney and Tom DeLay has already antagonized more traditional Republicans, as revealed in Ron Suskind's *The Price of Loyalty*. Bush/Cheney's reelection will strengthen the far right of the GOP, making the Republicans the chosen vehicle for a hard capitalist assault on all remnants of the New Deal. Mike Davis has correctly pointed out that "the real Achilles heel of the Democrats, in other words, is the economy, not morality. The biggest wedge issue in the coal and steel valleys is industrial decline, not the threat of gay monogamy."

The choice facing the Democrats is straightforward. Either they seriously oppose all this or they compete and offer a more refined Clintonesque version of the Republican package. Tony Blair did this to good effect by giving hard-nosed Thatcherism a cosmetic cleanup and labeling it the "third way." In the process he weakened the Conservative Party in Britain and replaced it with New Labour, which is currently in bed with the Republicans. But Clinton has already tried that in the States and it was only partially successful. It is unlikely to work again.

Nor will an alternative arise by uniting the disparate forces of the Greens and the far-left sects. The shift to the right in the recent election wiped out Nader as well. Given the winner-take-all basis of the electoral system, only a major crisis or a revival of mass resistance— involving sections of the unions—that leads to a serious split of the liberal intelligentsia from the rightward-moving Democrats in the Congress could start the foundation of a credible Third Party to the left of Clinton/Kerry. However desirable such a solution may be, it still seems a long way off. Meanwhile, all those who oppose the war and the social/economic/cultural agenda of the born-again Bush people have to remain in their posts and fight back. With the elections over, MoveOn needs to puts its name into practice and move on from elections to the campaign against the war in Iraq and demand the withdrawal of all U.S. troops.

The late Pham Van Duong, the prime minister of Vietnam, used to say that the road to Watergate lay through the jungles and cities of South Vietnam. History is an unpredictable creature, but perhaps change in the United States might come about because of what is happening in Fallujah and the labyrinths of Baghdad. Bush has won at home, but he might yet be defeated abroad. I hope so.

Tariq Ali
November 2004

Index